A Silvan Tomkins Handbook

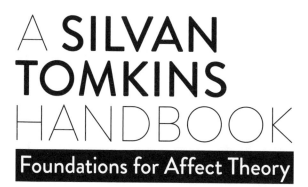

A SILVAN TOMKINS HANDBOOK
Foundations for Affect Theory

Adam J. Frank and Elizabeth A. Wilson

University of Minnesota Press
Minneapolis | London

This book is freely available in an open access edition thanks to TOME (Toward an Open Monograph Ecosystem)—a collaboration of the Association of American Universities, the Association of University Presses, and the Association of Research Libraries—and the generous support of Emory University and the Andrew W. Mellon Foundation. Learn more at the TOME website, available at: openmonographs.org.

Published by the University of Minnesota Press
111 Third Avenue South, Suite 290
Minneapolis, MN 55401-2520
http://www.upress.umn.edu

Printed in the United States of America on acid-free paper

The University of Minnesota is an equal-opportunity educator and employer.

27 26 25 24 23 22 21 20   10 9 8 7 6 5 4 3 2 1

Library of Congress Cataloging-in-Publication Data
Names: Frank, Adam J., author. | Wilson, Elizabeth A., author.
Title: A Silvan Tomkins handbook : foundations for affect theory / Adam J. Frank, Elizabeth A. Wilson.
Description: Minneapolis : University of Minnesota Press, 2020. | Includes bibliographical references and index. | Summary: "An accessible guide to the work of American psychologist and affect theorist Silvan Tomkins" —Provided by publisher.
Identifiers: LCCN 2020020378 (print) | ISBN 978-0-8166-7999-7 (hc) | ISBN 978-0-8166-8000-9 (pb)
Subjects: LCSH: Affect (Psychology) | Consciousness. | Personality. | Tomkins, Silvan S. (Silvan Solomon), 1911–1991.
Classification: LCC BF175.5.A35 F73 2020 (print) | DDC 152.4—dc23
LC record available at https://lccn.loc.gov/2020020378

FOR EKS

CONTENTS

NOTE ON QUOTATIONS

References in the text to Silvan Tomkins's four-volume work *Affect Imagery Consciousness* (New York: Springer, 1962–92) are given by the letters *AIC*, and quotations from these volumes are denoted by (volume:page). We quoted from this work extensively to convey a sense of Tomkins's prose style and thinking habits. In each chapter, we highlighted in bold phrases or sentences that communicate important ideas. All italics in these quotations are Tomkins's.

DEPARTMENT: PSYCHOLOGY   NAME: TOMKINS, Silvan S.

BORN: June 4, 1911

DEGREES:

    1930 B.A. University of Pennsylvania
    1931 M.A.   "   "   "
    1934 Ph.D.   "   "   "
NON-PRINCETON RECORD:

    1943-46   Harvard University - Inst
    1946-47   "   "   - Lect

PRINCETON RECORD:

    1947-48 Visiting Lecturer with rank o

Page from Silvan Tomkins's personnel file at Princeton University. Department of Rare Books and Special Collections, Princeton University Library, AC107, Box 524. Photograph by Orren Jack Turner.

INTRODUCTION

If you're reading this Introduction, there's a good chance that you would like to make sense of the work of the American psychologist Silvan Tomkins (1911–91). Perhaps you are a researcher seeking a handle on a complicated body of theory, a student who has encountered references to Tomkins in the classroom, or a clinician looking for a conceptual frame for the affects you encounter in the session. Maybe you are simply curious about the technical term *affect* as it has entered scholarly discourse in the humanities and social sciences and wonder what, exactly, this term means. We hope this handbook will serve as a resource that enables you to work with Tomkins's ideas in your own domain of interest. We have tried to provide a clear outline of his affect theory, otherwise difficult to extract in concise form from the four volumes of his lifework *Affect Imagery Consciousness (AIC)* (Springer, 1962–63 and 1991–92) and fifty years of journal publications. We have divided our book into three parts corresponding to the categories: "Affect," "Imagery," "Consciousness." Each is further divided into interlocking sections or modules that provide definitions of key terms, explain theoretical innovations, and sketch historical and conceptual contexts. The book is designed so that these sections may be read either sequentially or (if the reader prefers) out of sequence as a reference book. Our main goal has been to make Tomkins's work accessible, portable, and useful.

It should go without saying but we'll say it anyway: this handbook does not offer a substitute for the experience of reading Tomkins's work, which is far too rich and problematic for any adequate summation. We have pointed to places where the reader may wish to turn to the primary texts under discussion and have offered suggestions for further reading at the end of each section (including this Introduction). In other words, readers are encouraged to immerse themselves or dive in. We think of our book as a makeshift handrail that guides a reader gently into these strange waters, more hidden grotto than cement pool, with surprising drops and shallows, hot and cold spots, and strong currents that

1

can bring a swimmer, quite unexpectedly, into the open sea. We have learned first to wade and then to swim in these invigorating waters over twenty-five years of looking for handholds on slimy rocks and exploring nooks, crannies, and tide pools. We hope readers profit from our cartographic findings and that others can redraw these maps as they explore Tomkins's work in their own way.

But why, we hear some readers ask, spend so much time with a thinker whose work is so challenging or difficult? (We have especially heard the latter term used, calling to mind the phrase *a difficult child*.) The question could be asked of any number of speculative thinkers or theorists—everyone has his or her favorite punching bag. For many scholars in the critical humanities, Tomkins's particular difficulty has been its provenance in twentieth-century Anglo-American philosophy and psychology, which presents a rather different challenge than the figurative and grammatical densities associated with Continental philosophy. Tomkins's work offers an unpredictable, at times exhilarating mix of empirical and speculative accounts of psychological phenomena. Not unlike Freud, who drew on neuroanatomical and physiological studies to construct a wide-ranging phenomenological analysis of human psychology, Tomkins combines experimental protocols (clinical trials, large-scale surveys, projective tests) and high-level cross-disciplinary conceptualization, with all the risks this entails for reception, peer recognition, and intellectual uptake.

A more fundamental difficulty belongs to the main topic of his writing: affect itself. If Freud brought sexuality into the conceptual and clinical limelight, Tomkins wanted to refocus that light on affect (although, as we will see, by no means did he wish to exclude or sideline sexuality). And he chose to work, not within the cloisters of psychoanalysis, but from the perspective of an empirically oriented academic psychology. Although affect was not a taboo subject for mid-century psychology, it nonetheless posed a peculiar set of problems, primary among these being, how do you study it? What measurable physiological phenomena are reliably associated with affective experience? What role should introspective reports play in the study of affect? In addition to these questions of method, however, there is the prior, ideological question of whether affect *should* be studied. On one hand, many researchers in academic psychology have considered affect to be a hopelessly subjective set of phenomena properly suited to other, more speculative domains of study. Some years ago, one of us (E.W.) presented a brief appraisal of Tomkins's affect theory to a department of psychology. A colleague, seemingly both intrigued and aggravated by Tomkins's quasi-algorithmic formulation of shame as the incomplete reduction of the positive affects of interest or enjoyment, expostulated, "Yes. But you can't study shame in a rat!" On the other hand, for those who view affective experience in essentialist terms, either primarily as self-expression or private contact with a personal truth, to theorize affect is to risk blanching it, taking it away from experience via linguistic abstraction—feelings become disenchanted, hung out to dry. To put feelings into words, according to this perspective, is to contaminate both feelings and words, to betray them and oneself.

But if Freud has taught us anything, it is that self-betrayal is inevitable and that, in acts of self-betrayal, it becomes possible to attend to what he called "psychic reality," a reality that is neither easy to know nor entirely inaccessible. Tomkins's investigations of affect, like Freud's (and Spinoza's, as we suggest in the first interlude), posit the psyche (or mind) as a dynamic domain of the not-yet-known. Their therapeutics seek, not to restore an essential pregiven "self" to itself, but to develop a vocabulary that lets us name and begin to think about the multiple roles of affective experience in our lives. Consider the interesting fact that, like words, feelings both are and are not our own. For example, my joy at reuniting with a beloved is at once highly personal and idiosyncratic to me, and it also resembles the joy you would experience in a similar situation. And this is true even though our two experiences are, in other ways, quite unlike: my joy tends to be accompanied by a feeling of anger (at my beloved for leaving in the first place) and heart-dropping dread (that I will be left again), while yours is accompanied by an exciting mix of lust and jealousy. To put this another way, much of the time, we don't know, and don't want to know, what we are feeling. The assumption that feelings are vague, inarticulable, or ineffable can begin to sound more like a defense against acknowledging unwanted feelings than a persuasive account of experience. Or, to use Tomkins's own formulation, it is a decontamination script that maintains a strict boundary between word and feeling.

Tomkins's work navigates the complexities of these subjective and empirical demands by presenting affect as an umbrella category that can be characterized in the following terms:

neurological: Affects are defined, in his innate activator model, by a certain profile of neural firing.

physiological: Affects are delineated by sets of muscular, glandular, and skin responses.

aesthetic: The affects are experienced consciously as different feelings.

Though none of these has priority over the others, Tomkins's consistent phenomenology of the affects has brought our attention to the aesthetic, that is, what affects feel like in experience. He is careful to observe that affect is rarely experienced in its "pure" state. As amplifier of the drives and, more generally, part of a system of motivation that fuses with thoughts, perceptions, motor actions, drive states, and other affects, affective experience is almost always a blend. Consider, for example, how Tomkins understands emotions: these consist of one or more affects in combination with cognitive or drive states in a manner that colors, flavors, or inflects the affects. While anger-rage is one of Tomkins's primary affects, indignation is an emotion, as is fury, hatred, and scorn, each a somewhat distinct inflection of the affect anger-rage. Similarly, lust and curiosity both involve the affect interest-excitement, while the primary affect of shame-humiliation is at the core of the quite different emotions of shyness, embarrassment, and guilt. And so on. What Tomkins offers, then, is a periodic table of affective elements that combine to become any number of emotional molecular structures or substances. With this framework, we may begin to analyze affective experience into constituents as part of a dynamic inquiry into what's going on.

We note here that Tomkins's formulation of nine *primary* affects is not an argument for nine *sovereign* affects and that his claim that the affects are *innate* does not mean that they are predetermined or that they are separate from systems of meaning, purpose, signification, or sociality. We find ourselves disagreeing, therefore, strongly, with Ruth Leys's assessment that affects and cognitions are "two entirely separate systems" in Tomkins's work (*Ascent of Affect*, 19). While Leys is right to note that

Tomkins distinguishes between affects and cognition (and drives), she overreads the autonomy of these systems in his work and dismisses the dependencies and interdependencies that structure his cybernetically inflected account of human beings. According to Leys, Tomkins initiated a scholarly lineage (what she calls the anti-intentionalist stance of contemporary research on emotion) that splits affect from reason and that conceptualizes emotions as discrete, innate, automatically triggered events that operate independently of consciousness or meaning. This argument misses Tomkins's insistence on the intimate relation between affect and purpose, meaning, and value as such. We read Tomkins for his commitment to complexity, feedback, systematicity, contingency, and plurideterminacy: how affects and drives *together* form the basis of motivation (chapter 1); how cognitions become heated when coassembled with affects and, contrariwise, how affects become informed and smarter when coassembled with cognition (chapter 4); how affective scenes are magnified into scripts (chapter 9); how affects have evolved as mechanisms that are loosely matched to each other and to cognitive, perceptual, and motor mechanisms (chapter 12); and how affects are just one component of a "minding system" that is indissolubly cognitive and motivational (chapter 14).

One of our hopes for this handbook is that it will encourage researchers to read more deeply into Tomkins and perhaps find themselves differently oriented to the formulations of affect, biology, and sociality that have become conventional in the so-called affective turn. In particular, we are thinking of the work in affect studies that aligns itself primarily with Brian Massumi's influential interpretation of affect as (1) an impersonal intensity that operates independently of systems of signification or language and (2) an event that is configured differently from the sociolinguistic conventions of emotion: "emotion and affect . . . follow different logics and pertain to different orders" (88). Many scholars of affect after Massumi have preferred to read for the asignifying intensity of affect over the narrativized and individualized character of emotion. There can be considerable conceptual and political loss in this now-routinized critical stance. In trying to reformulate the kind of work that "affect" can do, affect studies often neglects subjective and intersubjective experience, for example. The pursuit of affectivity in the domain of the posthuman can sometimes leave the affective life of human worlds significantly undertheorized. As we have noted, Tomkins's affect theory also distinguishes between affect and emotion, but it does so without the ontological certainty of "different orders." Instead, it provides a conceptual framework for thinking about the nature of different affective states and their relation to other psychic, social, and biological events. It is, we believe, a cogent, complex, and generative theory of affect.

Tomkins's work is slowly moving into wider scholarly circulation, and there is increasing recognition that what is elaborated in his theory of affect remains important for critical thinking across a wide range of disciplines and interdisciplines. Certainly things have changed since Eve Kosofsky Sedgwick invited one of us (A.F.) to participate in a reading and writing project that issued in *Shame and Its Sisters: A Silvan Tomkins Reader* in 1995. It is gratifying to observe that what "theory knows today" (Sedgwick and Frank, 1) is not the same as what theory knew twenty-five years ago. In the rest of our Introduction, we would like to mark what has changed and how Tomkins's work is still valuable in a contemporary context.

First, the antibiologism that Sedgwick and Frank note had become an important point of departure for so many routines of theory in the humanities and social sciences is no longer so habitually deployed. This antibiologism once all but constituted the critical theories that were committed to antiessentialism and, what usually accompanied them, efforts to debunk or demystify the putatively natural. There has been ongoing and intensifying argument since 1995 that research in the humanities and social sciences might benefit from the integration of (or at least familiarity with) neurological or cognitive or genetic data. Not all these projects have been successful—some use scientific data too credulously—but theory no longer suspects that distance from biology is necessary for, or a guarantor of, critical or political engagement.

Second, language is no longer "assumed to offer the most productive, if not the only possible, models for understanding representation" (Sedgwick and Frank, *Shame and Its Sisters*, 1). Consider a particularly salient example: Michel Foucault's notion of *discourse* (by which he meant a collection of rules determining what can and cannot be said at a specific historical juncture) has been displaced by notions of media and mediation, that is, the technological substrata that determine what can and cannot be perceived or thought at a given juncture. One thinks of media theory as it emerges in the work of Friedrich Kittler and his interpreters. From a different angle, one may observe both a proliferation of nonlinguistic models of representation (picture theory, for example) and attempts to sideline representation as such (actor-network theory, thing theory). More generally, ontology now authorizes theory in a way that more epistemically focused approaches to language once did.

This leads directly to the third and fourth points that Sedgwick and Frank make: the seemingly urgent and interminable identification and dismantling of binarized structures as *the* core concern for an engaged critical practice. Today's critical projects (especially those that operate under the rubric of affect studies) are less attentive to the operations of binarized thinking. These theorists engage in ontological speculations that recast aesthetic, ethical, social, and material dynamics in the hope of offering (in some sense) better descriptions that create (in some sense) better performative consequences. The motives are often explicitly reparative, the methods speculative. There has been, if not a broadening, then certainly a reorientation of the methodological field, and there remains considerable ambiguity around the question of what criticism does and is for.

There is much in Tomkins's work that can contribute to these reconfigurations. We would remind readers that his work offers, not only a theory of affect, but theories of imagery and consciousness as well. Affect, imagery, and consciousness are inextricably entwined, for example, in his notion of *theory*, which weaves together epistemic and ontological concerns with questions of motivation. Recent criticism has been particularly drawn to his distinction between weak and strong theories (chapter 8). A strong theory is one that is able to account for large swaths of data and many eventualities. Psychoanalysis, especially in its classical Freudian forms, often makes use of strong theories (e.g., castration): it is able to engage, explain, and offer a conceptual infrastructure for a large archive of human behaviors, pleasures, fantasies, pathologies, and cultural productions. A weak theory, by contrast, has a much smaller compass. Its explanatory power is closely calibrated to the events at hand: a weak theory reads closely. Or, in the language of the clinic, it deals (effectively) with experience near data. Tomkins does not advocate for weak theories over strong ones, but he does draw our attention to the cost of strong theories: what is lost as well as gained in the strengthening of a given theory. As Deleuzian theories of affect become strong, for example, we find Tomkins's account of weak theory a helpful reminder of the importance of a methodological ecology that can support many, differently powerful ways of thinking about affect: not just Deleuzian or Tomkinsian but also psychoanalytic, phenomenological, Aristotelian, empirical, biochemical, and, of course, the myriad traditions of thinking about emotion beyond the West (in India, China, and North American indigenous cultures, for example).

We see as yet untapped critical utility in the theory of scenes (the contingent but possibly enduring attachment of an affect to an object) and scripts (the magnification of scenes into rules for the management of everyday feeling; chapter 9) and in his account of ideology as an organized set of ideas about which we are most passionate but also least certain (chapter 10). We find it significant that, in Tomkins's account, affect precedes value. Our ethical and political beliefs are rooted in scripts whose primary function is to guide and organize our affective scenes. These scripts, at once individual and social, emerge from a combination of disparate temporalities and spatialities (individual development, sociopolitical conflict, evolutionary inheritance). Consider how script theory offers resources for understanding the 2016 U.S. presidential campaign: as an exercise in summoning and manipulating varieties of (anti-)toxic resentment scripts pertaining to class, gender, and race. While some of these scripts are highly specific to local economic conditions, others are more loosely connected to the history of white supremacy in the United States, still others to misogynist demonology. Resentment, a complex emotion based on the affects of anger-rage and (what Tomkins calls) dissmell, may have many objects. Clearly Donald Trump's remarkably disinhibited expression of resentment and the enjoyment he and others take in these expressions served as a lightning rod for a great variety of resentments and the scripts that organize them. And, of course, resentment breeds resentment (similar dynamics appear to be governing the transnational resurgence of authoritarian "populisms," so called).

In addition to engaging with the particular innovations of Tomkins's theory, we are hoping that readers of this handbook will be able to rearrange the overly simplistic intellectual affiliations that have come to shape the field of affect studies. Many readers will have already noted that there is now a tendency to bifurcate affect studies into two traditions (the Darwinian and the Deleuzian, say) and then position these "traditions" agonistically, as if a critical choice is to be made. It seems to us that this structuring of the critical scholarship often duplicates a conventional division between mind and body (between signification and material, between discourse and affect), and so it has unwittingly intensified rather than alleviated the so-called two cultures problem. We have presented Tomkins's work here in a way that begins to complicate such easy intellectual divisions—there are important strands of influence in his work (see our interludes on Spinoza and Darwin) that do not conform to the taxonomies of what affect theory knows and feels today.

Tomkins's work remains compelling into the current century in part because we are in desperate need of a conceptualization of subjective experience that is, at the same time, open both to biological and sociopolitical domains. His deft use of cybernetics to think of humans as loosely fitted coassemblies of interrelated systems offers the beginning of one answer to this need (see chapter 12). Our contemporary moment is constrained by a set of knots or double-binds, perhaps the most powerful of which pertain to the strange status of subjectivity. We appear to be committed to epistemic perspectivalism (all knowledge is situated) at the same time that we reject subjectivity's role in constructing knowledge, as if the latter automatically entails irredeemable forms of solipsism or humanism. Faced with such oppositions and the near-intolerable anxieties they breed, the middle grounds of feeling and thinking that comprise everyday knowledge and experience tend to go missing. Tomkins's work lets us begin to find and make space for these middle grounds.

FURTHER READING

We recommend a handful of essays that will help orient readers to the so-called affective turn. Melissa Gregg and Gregory Seigworth's introduction to *The Affect Theory Reader* gives an overview of the field, although Tomkins is mentioned only in passing and is not much taken up by other contributors to the anthology. Russ Leo ("An Archive for Affect Theory") has reviewed the volume in ways we have found very helpful. Constantina Papoulias and Felicity Callard ("Biology's Gift: Interrogating the Turn to Affect") and Clare Hemmings ("Invoking Affect: Cultural Theory and the Ontological Turn") have been strongly critical of affect theory. They discuss Tomkins more than most overviews of the field, but these discussions still rely more on secondary sources than they do on a direct engagement with Tomkins's texts. The special issue of *Body and Society* edited by Lisa Blackman and Couze Venn (16, no. 1 [2010]) and Patricia Tincento Clough's anthology *The Affective Turn* investigate how the study of affect reorganizes scholarship on embodiment.

Since Sedgwick and Frank's critique of a routinized antibiologism in 1995 ("Shame in the Cybernetic Fold: Reading Silvan Tomkins"), numerous influential texts, especially in feminist theory, have developed ways to think with the data from the biological and natural sciences (e.g., Barad's *Meeting the Universe Halfway,* Bennett's *Vibrant Matter,* Malabou's *What Should We Do with Our Brain?*). For an excellent accounting of how neuroscientific data have been used with varying degrees of success in the social sciences, see Des Fitzgerald and Felicity Callard ("Social Science and Neuroscience beyond Interdisciplinarity: Experimental Entanglements").

We have already put down our thoughts, in more detail, about the ways in which Leys misreads Tomkins's affect theory. We refer readers interested in that debate to the 2011 and 2012 issues of *Critical Inquiry* that contain Leys's original article, our response, and her rejoinder (37, no. 3; 38, no. 4). We refer readers not yet acquainted with Brian Massumi's influential account of affect to *Parables for the Virtual: Movement, Affect, Sensation* (and especially "The Autonomy of Affect") in the first instance.

PART I
AFFECT

1
DRIVES

"Drive Theory Is Dead." This is the provocative title that Silvan Tomkins gave to the first presentation of his nascent affect theory. The talk was delivered sometime in the early 1950s to "the stronghold of Freudian and Hullian drive theory" at Yale University (4:xiv). Tomkins reports that (surprisingly) the paper was well received and that he presented it again at the International Congress of Psychology in Montreal in 1954. Looking for a publisher for this paper, he was rejected by every journal of psychology in the United States. Eventually, with the help of the psychoanalyst Daniel Lagache, the paper was published, in French, in a 1956 anthology edited by Jacques Lacan. Other contributors to this volume *(La Psychoanalyse)* are Emile Benveniste, Martin Heidegger, Jean Hyppolite, Daniel Lagache, Eliane Amado Lévy-Valensi, Clémence Ramnoux, and Lacan himself. This story may seem peculiar to the contemporary reader—it may seem odd that the same paper could find an amicable reception from both behaviorists and psychoanalysts; it may be surprising that a mid-century American psychologist could place his work in a volume alongside Continental philosophers, analysts, and semioticians. Nonetheless, this story is a useful way to approach Tomkins's work. We will argue that his affect theory is notable for how it engages tenets of behaviorism, psychoanalysis, and (eventually) cognitivism to build a different (indeed, provocative) kind of psychological theory. By being interested in each of these schools, yet affixed to none, Tomkins was able to generate a brilliant, idiosyncratic, and complex understanding of the affect system informed as much by cybernetics and systems theory as by psychoanalysis, neuropsychology, learning theory, ethology, and studies of perception and cognition.

When Tomkins first began thinking and writing about affect, psychological theory in the United States was dominated by two schools: behaviorism and psychoanalysis. While these schools are usually positioned antagonistically in relation to key clinical and conceptual tenets (the status of unconscious mental processes being perhaps the most infamous), Tomkins argued for their convergence. He suggested that there is one important way in which behaviorism and psychoanalysis were compatible: both schools take *drives* to be the motivating forces of human psychology. For the behaviorist, a person is motivated to act (or not) in relation to the conditioning of drive states (hunger being paradigmatic). For the psychoanalyst, a person is motivated, unconsciously, by the vicissitudes of sexual drives (the perversion of hunger into orality being paradigmatic). Even though J. B. Watson's (1920) earliest experiments with conditioning were structured by the manipulation of fear, and even though Freud's (1895) first cases of hysteria were notable for their descriptions of emotional lability, each tradition eventually placed more explanatory weight on drive gratification than affective experience. Tomkins argued that one of the effects of this dominance of drive theory is that neither behaviorism nor psychoanalysis is able fully to attend to how affects work as motivators. This has further consolidated the subordinate status of the affects in psychological theory: "Historically, many have regarded the affects not only as secondary to the drives but even as the prime disorganizers . . . something of a bull in a china shop of man's organized repertoire of responses" (1:40).

One of Tomkins's first gestures as he begins *AIC* is to reorganize this logic. Putting aside the instinctual inclinations of both behaviorism and psychoanalysis, he argues that affects are the primary motivators of human behavior: we act (learn, think, remember, crave, attach) in relation to fear or surprise, enjoyment or shame. While it appears that humans are motivated by drive states (breathing, thirst, defecation, hunger, sex, pain), much of this motivational power has been "borrowed" (1:22) from the affect system. Tomkins argued that drives, on their own, are surprisingly weak motivators of action; they provide information about motivation but very little impetus to actually move. The drives have psychological power only to the extent that they are amplified by the affects: **"The affect system is therefore the primary motivational system because without its amplification, nothing else matters—and with its amplification, anything else can matter"** (3:6).

What, then, is the nature of this amplificatory relation between affects and drives? In the first instance, an affect has the effect of making a drive state *urgent*. In the neonate, for example, the affect of distress makes "hunger appear more urgent and harder to tolerate. The total distress is certainly greater than if there were hunger alone" (1:49). Hunger is motivating for a human—urging her or him to action—only when amplified by affects like distress, anger, excitement, or fear. For Tomkins, hunger urges, presses, or drives—in ways that matter—only when coassembled with an affect. Similarly for the sex drive, it too requires the amplification of an affect to be reconstituted as what we call sexuality: "Ordinarily the urgency of this drive is amplified by the affective response of interest or excitement. The sexual organ is the site of sexual pleasure, but the thrill of sexuality is more affect than specific sexual pleasure" (1:55). The affective thrill of sexuality need not always be tied to the positivity of excitement; it may also come from the amplifying effects of negative affects like fear or anger. Or, more interesting still, fear and excitement may jointly modulate the sex drive:

> Fear, united with sexual drive pleasure, is also capable of increasing the urgency and intensity of the sex drive. This is the lure of the tabooed and the forbidden, a complex combination of primary drive pleasure and positive and negative affect amplification. Negative affect amplification is here accompanied by the positive affective response of excitement which along with sexual pleasure gives the entire complex a predominantly positive tone. (1:57)

In these examples, we see the affective intensification of a drive: hunger becomes pressing, sex becomes fervent. And we should note that amplification, in Tomkins's theory, can be a complex combinatorial event—multiple affects can be activated in relation to one drive, and positive and negative affects may cohabit experientially. Moreover, affects can downwardly modulate a drive—masking, reducing, or inhibiting it. Disgust, fear, and distress can all attenuate the hunger drive; in the case of anorexia, this attenuation can be chronic and life threatening. Likewise, the sex drive can be significantly diminished by shame or fear or anger, making sex for Tomkins "the most finicky of drives" (4:xiii).

So the drives and the affects are different systems for Tomkins: they are differently configured biologically, and they have different psychological effects. One of the key ways in which affects and drives differ is that drives are biologically *specific,* whereas affects are *general.* That is, drives provide precise information about where to act (in the case of the hunger drive, here, in the mouth), when to act (sometime in the next few hours), what to do (eat), and the things to which we should be responsive (carbohydrates, fats, proteins). That is, the drive tells quite a specific story about how, when, and where it is to be consummated. In the case of hunger, the drive is a biological mechanism particular to the mouth and stomach, and it can best be satisfied by food. Orality, leaning on this hunger mechanism, is similarly specific in Freudian psychoanalysis—it cleaves to the mouth and is satisfied by oral stimulation. Tomkins would argue that while the varieties of food and methods of oral stimulation may be extensive, elaborate, and perverse, the biological specificity of the hunger drive remains the focal point of such theories. In both cases, the hunger drive demands attention to (and gratification from) a specific bodily site. As a way of demonstrating that specificity of the drive, Tomkins proposes a thought experiment:

> Let us suppose that the hunger drive were "rewired" to be localized in the urethra and the sex drive localized in the palm of the hand. For sexual satisfaction the individual would first open and close his hand and then reach for a wide variety of "objects" as possible satisfiers, cupping and rubbing his hands until orgasm. When he became hungry, he might first release the urethra and urinate to relieve his hunger. If this did not relieve it, he might use his hands to find objects which might be put inside the urethra, depending on just how we rewired the apparatus. Such an organism would be neither viable nor reproductive. Such specificity of time and place of the drive system, critical though it is for the viability, is, nevertheless, a limitation on its general significance for the human being. ("Affect Theory," 356–57)

Drives have a clarity to them: we tend to know where we are hungry or thirsty or in pain, and we tend to be able to distinguish fairly reliably between drive states (between, say, being hungry and being sexually aroused, between the need to breathe and the need to defecate). This particularity of the drives, Tomkins argues, is what limits their significance for psychological action.

There is usually much less clarity about affects—about what they are, how many there are, or where they are. It is commonplace that I might not know whether I am afraid or excited or angry, I might not know when my excitement has become anger, and I am unlikely to be able to say where these experiences are happening or how they might be reliably up- or down-regulated. This is what Tomkins calls the generality of the affects. This generality comes in a variety of forms:

- Affects are general in relation to *time*. Where the temporality of hunger is somewhat contained (eat now!) and becomes increasingly urgent within a fairly short period of time, the affects have highly variable temporalities: "one can be anxious for just a moment or for half an hour, or for a day, or for a month, or for a year, a decade or a lifetime, or *never* or only occasionally now though much more frequently than some time ago" (1:172).

- Affects are general in relation to *bodily location*: excitement, for example, has no necessary affiliation to a body part in the way that hunger does to the stomach, or defecation to the bowel.

- Affects are general in relation to the *responses* they demand: there is often no easily identifiable way to reduce my fear in the way that eating fairly reliably reduces hunger. I may develop strategies for reducing fear, but likely I also know, through bitter experience, that such strategies are liable to break down and I will need to keep reinventing new tactics to keep my fear at bay.

- Crucially, affects are general in relation to *objects*: "any affect may have any 'object'" (1:347). The drive–object relations that Freud (1915) elaborated in terms of the vicissitudes of the instincts Tomkins reorganizes as affect–object freedom: "**there is literally no kind of object that has not been linked to one or another of the affects**" ("Affect Theory," 358).

The early chapters of *AIC* elucidate this important distinction between drives and affects. However, as soon as this distinction is in place, Tomkins begins to rework it. Pain, for example, seems to be midway between an affect and a drive; it has a generality of time, for example, but not of bodily location. Moreover, some affects are intimately aligned with one particular drive, undermining a crisp distinction between affect and drive. The affect of disgust, for example, is auxiliary to the hunger drive. The turning of the head that is indicative of a disgusted response to bad food is also the affective response of disgust that signals rejection to the other and to the self.

This making and unmaking of a primary distinction between affects and drives, we argue, is one of the gestures that gives Tomkins's theory its uniquely compelling character. It allows him to build a psychological theory that values systematicity—the combinatorial dependencies, interdependencies, and independencies of various elements of mind. This relationality is one of the threads in Tomkins's thinking that we will make legible throughout this book. Here we simply note that, for Tomkins, an affect is not a singular, hardwired event. It is a systemic occurrence composed of neural firing, facial musculature, glandular messages, motor responses, memory, images, sensory and perceptual feedback, and affect "accretions" (1:244). As we remember that an affect is coassembled with drives (amplifying drives, but also possibly being activated by them), with cognitions, with other affects, and with other neurological systems (what Tomkins called auxiliary amplifying systems), we can see both the scope of Tomkins's theory and the difficulty that any reader might have in trying to comprehend it:

> We began our examination of the drive system with the assumption that what had passed for drive for centuries was in fact a drive–affect assembly. We shall end this examination of both systems with a glimpse of an ever-changing multi-component set of drives, affects, general and specific amplifiers and attenuators. These, along with the transmuting mechanism which transforms messages into conscious form, and the perceptual and memory systems enter into the ever-changing central assemblies, to be described later, which govern the human organism. (1:88)

The identity of affects and drives, and the distinctiveness of their allegedly essential characteristics, begins to look more contingent as *AIC* unfolds. Because affects on their own can motivate behavior, and because drives require the amplifying influence of affects to impel action, one might be led to think that affects themselves are the primary source of motivation. Against this idea of affective sovereignty or autonomy,

Tomkins argues that it is the combinatorial assemblages of affects and drives that have psychological efficacy: "the primary motivational units are the drive–affect combinations" (1:65). That is, Tomkins flips the conventional status of affects and drives, not to banish drives or to unequivocally favor affects, but to join them to each other more potently.

FURTHER READING

The second chapter of *AIC1* ("Drive–Affect Interactions: Motivational Information of Time and Place of Response—When, Where, What, to What") has a detailed account of the relation between drives and affects. We also relied on some later chapters in *AIC1* for further elaboration of the relation between affects and drives: see chapter 6 ("Visibility and Invisibility of the Affect System," especially pages 171–86) and chapter 8 ("The Innate Determinants of Affect," especially pages 249–58).

The relation between Tomkins and psychoanalysis will be a continuing concern for us in this book. We refer readers interested in how Freud elaborates the relations of objects to drives to his canonical paper "Instincts and Their Vicissitudes." For Freud on the perversion of the drives, we recommend his earlier work on infantile sexuality and polymorphous perversity ("Three Essays on the Theory of Sexuality").

The relation between Tomkins's work and the psychoanalytic scene in Paris in the 1950s has not yet been explored. Daniel Lagache attended the 1954 International Congress of Psychology and was, at the same time, a close colleague of Lacan. According to Tomkins, it was Lagache who initiated the publication of Tomkins's paper in French. Lagache, who would oversee the writing of the canonical *Language of Psychoanalysis* by Jean Laplanche and Jean-Bertrand Pontalis, was always interested in the integration of psychoanalysis and psychology—a task that Elisabeth Roudinesco in her partisan account of Lagache, Lacan, and the Société française de psychanalyse calls "impossible" (215). The 1956 volume *La Psychoanalyse. 1. Travaux des Années 1953–1955* is a publication of the Société française de psychanalyse. When presented to the International Congress of Psychology, Tomkins's paper was titled "Consciousness and the Unconscious in a Model of the Human Being"; in the 1956 volume, the title is "La conscience et l'inconscient répresentes dans une modéle de l'être humain."

2
THE FACE

In 2009, Fox television aired the pilot episode of *Lie to Me,* a crime procedural drama whose hero, played by a perpetually undershaven Tim Roth, is an expert in emotional expression. Dr. Cal Lightman's uncanny ability to determine whether a person is lying is based on his knowledge of "microexpressions," fast, easy-to-miss movements of facial (and other) muscles that, he claims, indicate what a person is really feeling. The show makes its underlying premise clear with great economy in an early scene that has Lightman lecturing in front of an initially skeptical, then quickly appreciative audience of U.S. defense and security workers. In answer to the question "don't these microexpressions vary depending on the person?" he shows a set of slides displaying people of different ages, genders, and races, in a variety of situations, but with similar expressions of scorn, shame, sadness, joy, and so on. "These expressions are universal," he intones as the slides (and music) slam home his point. "Emotion looks the same whether you're a suburban housewife or a suicide bomber. The truth is written on all our faces" ("Pilot").

These premises—that emotions may be revealed visually via facial microexpressions, and that at least some emotional expressions are universal—are based on the research program of Paul Ekman, a psychologist at the University of San Francisco who has been studying emotion and facial behavior since the 1960s and who has become both prominent and controversial in the field. Part of the controversy surrounding Ekman comes from his techniques of self-promotion: he has made his research available outside the academy through the Paul Ekman Group, which advertises the Micro Expressions Training Tool on its website and offers a sequence of deception training courses (used by the U.S. Transportation Security Administration and other law enforcement). Samuel Baum, the playwright who created *Lie to Me,* spent a year going through Ekman's deception training program and hired the psychologist as a consultant on the show. Ekman's courses and train-ing tools are based on the Facial Action Coding System (FACS), first published in 1978 (since updated and reissued in digital format). FACS is a rigorous, complex, and exhaustive taxonomical analysis of the move-ments of facial musculature and the expressive capacities of the human face that Ekman developed with William Friesen.

In 1971 Ekman, Friesen, and Tomkins coauthored "Facial Affect Scoring Technique: A First Validity Study," an early precursor to FACS (the acronym was FAST). Ekman has long acknowledged the relation-ship between his work and Tomkins's. The two first met in the mid-1960s after Ekman read Tomkins's article (coauthored with Robert McCarter) "What and Where Are the Primary Affects? Some Evidence for a Theory" (1964). Impressed with this study's results and the evidence it offered for a handful of innate, biologically based affects expressed primarily as facial behavior, Ekman began a series of cross-cultural stud-ies that aimed to demonstrate the universality of what he would later call the basic emotions. Ekman's interest in Tomkins's work was highly selective: he left aside much of the older psychologist's theory of affect, motivation, and personality to concentrate instead on the visibility and universality of expressive behavior. In fact, in moving from FAST to FACS, Ekman and Friesen left out affect altogether, replacing *facial affect* with *facial action*. While Tomkins's work has at times been as-similated with Ekman's, we would emphasize the significant differences between their methods, ideas, and scientific sensibilities. By contrast with Ekman's avoidance of theory and wholehearted commitment to strong empiricism, Tomkins's systematic, wide-ranging, at once specula-tive and empirical approach was not well received in the narrow, studies-oriented ethos that came to orient the discipline of academic psychology (we have more to say about Ekman in chapter 3).

In the context of these differences, consider that Tomkins con-sistently emphasized both the visibility of facial affect and its strange *in*-visibility. The chapter in *AIC1* titled "Visibility and Invisibility of the Affect System" begins with the "paradox" that despite their "pri-mary motivational significance" (1:171), the affects are not nearly as well known as the drives. Tomkins begins to account for this relative invisi-bility by describing the generality of affect with respect to time, place, response, and object (see chapter 1). For example, in a discussion of the

generality of place, he points out that, while "the site of the drive signal is also the site of the consummatory response" (1:174) (we experience hunger in the mouth and stomach, which we then fill by eating,
say), affects are "capable of being combined with numerous alternative
sub-assemblies, so that **phenomenologically the affect may be fused
with any type of experience**" (1:175). Tomkins uses two metaphors to
describe the "great combinatorial capacity of the affective system, its
ability to 'fuse' with other components" (1:175) and go unnoticed. The
first is linguistic: "Just as a letter loses some of its visibility as it enters
into different words, or a word into different sentences, so the affects
lose some of their uniqueness and visibility by virtue of their flexibility
of assembly" (1:175). Literary critics and other humanists may recognize
this metaphor in the thematics of the purloined letter made famous
through readings of Poe's tale of that name by Lacan, Derrida, and
others. Tomkins's implication is that affects hide in plain sight but may
become objects of analysis if an observer sees them as part of a spectrum
of elements that combine to create larger wholes.

Like other mid-century structuralist thinkers, Tomkins invokes language as a figure for ordered complexity and generative systems (see chapter 12). But he proposes another metaphor, a mixed chemical–anatomical
metaphor, to describe the peculiar invisibility of affect: "Because affects
are phenomenologically so soluble in every kind of psychic solution we
must expect that the distillation of purified components will be rarely
achieved by the individual who experiences the totality and pose formidable problems for the psychological anatomist who would dissect
and separate the components" (1:175). A chemical solution must be acted
upon with effort to effect a separation or purification of its component
parts. Tomkins implies that such a "distillation" or analysis of affect is
possible, but may do violence to its object. He makes use of this chemical
metaphor several times in his writing, returning to it in his last public
lecture in a call for more dynamic or integrative experimental protocols:
"We have a great craft union tendency to polarize and to debate things
which nature has put together, and to pull them asunder for analytic
experimental purposes. . . . We can tease them apart, we can factor them,
we can centrifuge them, but they [i.e., feelings] remain a unitary phenomenon, which exhibits many diverse characteristics at once. Now that

is not fashionable in science. It is called contamination. Unfortunately, we are deeply contaminated creatures" ("Inverse Archaeology," 285).

For Tomkins, the empirical study of affect requires experimental techniques that can accommodate rather than rule out complexity and contamination of both object and analyst. The generality of affect, the learned "transformations" (habituation, miniaturization, accretion, delay, avoidance), the taboos on looking at the face, and the problem of naming the emotions all make it difficult to perceive affects and tease them apart from other psychic phenomena. Equally important is the idea that affective response does not necessarily accompany affect awareness: "With affects it is not at all exceptional that one may respond and be unaware that one is angry, afraid, ashamed, excited, happy, or distressed. **Unconscious feeling means no more or less than unconscious hearing**" (1:186). This gap between response and awareness may distinguish Tomkins's theory of affect from the James–Lange theory, which defines emotion as the secondary awareness of physiological response, or as James famously put it in his essay "What Is an Emotion?," "our feeling of the same [bodily] changes as they occur IS the emotion" (189–90). By contrast, Tomkins suggests, "there are conscious reports of affect which do not necessarily emanate from peripheral facial or autonomic responses. Just as one may dream visual images without sensory stimulation, so one may emit central images of affective responses with or without facial or gross autonomic consequences" (1:187). We will return to these ideas in our discussion of Tomkins's notion of imagery (in chapter 7). For now, we would simply point to the important gap between affective experience (the feeling of anger, say) and response (such as a raised voice), a gap that makes it difficult to identify affect based on either self-report or other-directed observation.

Despite the many obstacles to identifying and analyzing affect, Tomkins begins the next chapter, "The Primary Site of the Affects: The Face," with this claim: "the primary affects, before the transformations due to learning, seem to be innately related in a one-to-one fashion with an organ system which is extraordinarily visible" (1:204). Hedging his bet ("seem to be"), Tomkins nonetheless proposes an indexical relation between the affects and the "organ system" of the face. Think of it this way: as the lungs are the primary organ of respiration and the heart the primary organ of the circulation of the blood, so is the face the primary organ of affective motivation. This focus on the face distinguishes Tomkins's theory from the James–Lange account, which emphasizes visceral or internal bodily response:

> We regard the relationship between the face and the viscera as analogous to that between the fingers, forearm, upper arm, shoulders, and body. The finger does not "express" what is in the forearm, or shoulder or trunk. It rather leads than follows the movements in these organs to which it is an extension. Just as the fingers respond both more rapidly with more precision and complexity than the grosser and slower moving arm to which they are attached, so the face expresses affect, both to others, and to the self, via feedback, which is more rapid and more complex than any stimulation of which the slower moving visceral organs are capable. (1:205)

Primarily behavior of the skin and muscles of the face and only secondarily visceral behavior, affect is communicated both outwardly (to others) and inwardly (to the self). "When we become aware of these facial and/or visceral responses we are aware of our affects. We may respond with these affects however without becoming aware of the feedback from them. Finally, we learn to generate, from memory, images of these same responses which we can become aware of with or without repetition of facial, skeletal or visceral responses" (1:206).

Note the complexity of Tomkins's account, which does not preclude the gut (or any other bodily location) as a site of affective response. This approach to the face and facial feedback respatializes the bodily network in a manner distinct from Freud's approach to the drives and their consummatory sites, although not necessarily in contradiction to it. Tomkins's respatialization begins with the face as most prominent in the body image, an idea he discusses in the context of a gruesome thought experiment: "If it were possible to amputate the face and for the subject to continue to live, we would predict a phantom face of much greater longevity and resistance to deformation and extinction than in the case of phantom limbs following amputation" (1:208). After observing that "the hand acts as if the face were the site of feeling" (1:210), Tomkins considers several examples of manual facial nurture and support (eye rubbing in fatigue, screening the face in shame), emphasizes the role of the hand in distress (finger sucking, cigarette smoking), and concludes that "much of the 'oral' complex is facial rather than strictly oral, just as some of the facial complex is bodily rather than strictly facial" (1:211). Consider how his discussion of "the face of the other as a goal" offers a revised idea of the psychoanalytic superego or ego-ideal: "The voice of conscience I am suggesting is the voice of a particular face who, in addition to speaking, is angry or shocked or disgusted or disappointed" (1:220). Rather than the consequence of an inward turn, a repression or internalization that creates the subject *tout court,* conscience is recast as a set of images or goals (conscious or not), phantom faces and voices that create a network of affectively structured, relational subjectivities. Phantom imagery (again, see chapter 7) recasts the psychoanalytic unconscious in cybernetic terms, rerouting the individuated subject through facial feedback aimed both inward and outward, motivating selves and others at once.

We will return to Tomkins's negotiations between the insights of psychoanalysis and the research methods of American academic psychology in a later chapter (chapter 11). Here we note how his commitment to complexity does not itself mitigate against an empirical research program like Ekman's. For example, in a discussion of the complexity of facial information, Tomkins returns to the linguistic metaphor and the need for the child to learn "the language of the face" (1:216). This metaphor underlies Ekman's attempt to codify a universal facial language, even while troubling it in insisting on the necessarily "somewhat culture-bound" nature of these perceptual skills: "The individual who moves from one class to another or one society to another is faced with the challenge of learning new 'dialects' of facial language to supplement his knowledge of the more universal grammar of emotion" (1:216). But Tomkins subtly changes his metaphor, turning to reading and writing as they figure the perceptual skills of translation, not between different "dialects" of facial language, but between different sensory modalities that contribute to affect awareness:

> This skill in interpreting the facial expression of others is aided or hindered by an isomorphism between the visual face of the other and the interoceptive face of the self. Although the feedback from

our own face is in non-visual modalities, we learn the rules of translation between what the face looks like to what it feels like and from both of these to the motor language, so that eventually we are capable of imitating either what a face looks like or what it feels like. In this way we become capable of putting on masks. . . . These rules of translation between the motor, visual and kinesthetic languages are analogous to the way in which we learn to write as we listen to a lecture or read a book, or as a mute person learns to speak with his fingers. (1:216–17)

The mute person speaking with his fingers is a figure for speech as writing. To make the deconstructive point explicit, the metaphor of writing foregrounds a dynamic temporal horizon that interferes with any empiricist effort to create a static, purely spatial taxonomy. At the same time that Tomkins proposes a universal grammar of emotion, he insists that the ability to use this grammar is necessarily conditioned by an observer's idiosyncratic history of affect, analogized to her history of learning to read and write, that is, to translate between the face of others and that of the self. Tomkins offers a host of examples of how the isomorphism between the face of the self and the face of the other can inflect the perception of affect or contaminate the study of affect because of the observer's own affective history.

Tomkins discusses such idiosyncratic histories by way of what he calls *facial styles.* He begins by suggesting that speech can directly compete with affect awareness: "Language interaction is usually so demanding and obtrusive that few individuals may penetrate the linguistic envelope to isolate the idiosyncratic style of the face of the other during conversation. For the student of affect, however, **if he will turn off the flow of information from linguistic interaction and attend simply to the face of the other, there is immediately revealed an astonishingly personal and simple style of affective facial behavior**" (1:223). Tomkins suggests tuning out speech to attend to facial style, or what in an earlier historical moment would have been called character. These "simple" facial styles are consequences of interactions between multiple, irreducibly temporal affective and cognitive components and thus index a fundamental complexity:

Facial style may represent fragments of facial goals, reactions to past success or failure in achieving these goals, and reactions to the expected outcome of instrumental behavior in pursuit of future facial goals. These distinguishable components may in combination produce a resultant facial expression which is difficult to identify since it represents part goal, part expectation of outcome of instrumental activity, part reaction to the past, part reaction to the present and part expectation of the future. It is not infrequent that a face is half sad from past distress and half excited at future prospects. (1:222–23)

One implication of Tomkins's emphasis on facial styles and the accompanying temporality and complexity of affect is that the pure or simple expression of individual affect is rare (except, perhaps, in infants and children). This offers another pointed contrast to Ekman's emphasis on emotion's visibility.

Tomkins's chapter on the face ends with a long summary of anatomical and physiological work, emphasizing the nineteenth-century neurologist G. B. Duchenne's *Mécanisme de la physionomie humaine, ou analyse electro-physiologique de l'expression des passions* (1862). Tomkins's review of hundred-year-old findings seems to have inspired Ekman, whose FACS updates Duchenne's work using different techniques to isolate facial muscles and nerves (Duchenne used electrical stimulation on a man who suffered from facial anesthesia). Famously, Darwin used several photographs from Duchenne's work to illustrate *The Expression of the Emotions in Man and Animals* (1872), edited by Ekman for Oxford University Press in 1998. Tomkins clearly differentiates his work from Ekman's in the third, much later volume of *AIC* (1991). There he describes the modifications he has made to his theory, including his reassessment of the skin of the face rather than its musculature as "of the greatest importance in producing the feel of affect" (3:10). He references his own work with McCarter as both "gratifying" and "somewhat misleading in overemphasizing the role of innately patterned facial muscular responses in the production of affect" (3:10), distancing his current thinking from Ekman's FACS approach. He also expresses skepticism concerning Ekman's argument that the primary evolutionary function of the face is to communicate affect: "My intuition was, and still is, that the communication of affect is a secondary spin-off function rather than the primary function" as a source of motivating feedback (3:11).

By the 1980s, Tomkins was dissatisfied with the uses made of his theory: "The radical increase in numbers of grant applications, papers, and book manuscripts in affect theory and research I have recently refereed testifies that the next decade or so belongs to affect. Having waited twenty years for this development, I am less than euphoric at what I see. It had been my hope that such a development might transform American psychology. Instead, the field of affect is, in part, being co-opted by the very fields it should have illuminated" (3:39). His own methodological commitments to complexity, synthesis, and discovery left him impatient with experimentalists who would test simplified versions of his theory. He continued to insist on a complex and contaminated cybernetic understanding of the motivating role of facial feedback for any adequate theory of affect.

FURTHER READING

Our discussion is largely based on two chapters from *AIC1,* "Visibility and Invisibility of the Affect System" (chapter 6) and "The Primary Site of the Affects: The Face" (chapter 7), as well as Tomkins's essays collected in *Exploring Affect* ("Part III: The Face of Affect") and introduced by Paul Ekman: "What and Where Are the Primary Affects? Some Evidence for a Theory" (with Robert McCarter), "The Phantasy behind the Face," and "Inverse Archaeology: Facial Affect and the Interfaces of Scripts within and between Persons" (plenary address given by Tomkins at the annual meeting of the International Society for Research on the Emotions in 1990).

We consulted several edited and coedited volumes by Ekman, including *Emotion in the Human Face* (1982), *Approaches to Emotion* (1984), *The Nature of Emotion* (1994), and *What the Face Reveals* (1997). Malcolm Gladwell's *New Yorker* article "The Naked Face" quotes Ekman's oft-repeated, heroizing anecdote about Tomkins's remarkable skills at reading facial affect from the films Ekman had taken of two distinct groups of indigenous peoples in New Guinea. We note that this anecdote seriously underestimates what Tomkins considers the invisibility of affect due to its complexity, transformations, and temporal dynamics.

For more on William James's theory of emotion, see "What Is an Emotion?" and the revised chapter in *Principles of Psychology*. It can be difficult to determine the precise relationship between James's account of emotion and Tomkins's in part because James's writing on this subject is not highly elaborated. By comparison with later cognitivist accounts, we would situate Tomkins's theory of affect in the Jamesian tradition, although we suspect that it is more specifically compatible with the Cannon–Bard model.

Finally, for a discussion of the thematics of the purloined letter, please see Edgar Allan Poe's "The Purloined Letter" and the essays collected in *The Purloined Poe*.

3
EVOLUTION

In the prior chapter, as we discussed the importance of the face for Tomkins's affect theory, it became clear that evolution is a central concern in his work. Indeed, it has become commonplace to talk about Tomkins in the context of the biological and psychological tradition that begins with Charles Darwin's *The Expression of the Emotions in Man and Animals* in 1872. In that book, Darwin shows that the emotional expressions we see in humans can also be found in the wider animal kingdom. There is nothing uniquely defining about the anger, fear, joy, or disgust that humans manifest; these are capacities given by evolutionary descent. There is a kinship, for example, between the bared teeth of an attacking, enraged primate and the snarl of human anger: "our semi-human progenitors uncovered their canine teeth when prepared for battle, as we still do when feeling ferocious, or when merely sneering at or defying someone" (251–52). At the time of publication, the scandal of this argument was that it tied humans more closely to animals than to God, rendering the human naturally rather than divinely made. These days, Darwin's work on emotion circulates in discussions, no less fraught, about the biological underpinnings of human psychology: How much human emotion is innate and predetermined? How much learned? Are human emotions universal? In particular, Darwin is frequently cited as the progenitor of the idea, now to be found in some psychological and neurological literatures, that there is a small range of basic emotional responses in humans that have been inherited from animal ancestors. The neuroscientist Jaak Panksepp, for example, nominates seven such affective systems: SEEKING, FEAR, RAGE, LUST, CARE, PANIC/GRIEF, PLAY. We will let his account of the infrastructure of mind stand as a typical articulation of this contemporary view about evolution and emotion:

To the best of our knowledge, the basic biological values of all
mammalian brains were built upon the same basic plan, laid out in
consciousness-creating affective circuits that are concentrated in
subcortical regions, far below the neocortical "thinking cap" that
is so highly developed in humans. Mental life would be impossible
without this foundation. There, among the ancestral brain networks
we share with other mammals, a few ounces of brain tissue consti-
tute the bedrock of our emotional lives, generating the many primal
ways in which we can feel emotionally good or bad within ourselves.
(*Archaeology of Mind*, 1)

Primal, ancestral, ancient, bedrock. Evolution is deployed here to argue
that human emotions are grounded in more or less fixed prehistoric
capacities. These so-called basic emotions anchor human minds in the
distant animalistic past, they are shared by all members of the species
Homo sapiens, and they are reliably (involuntarily) triggered by the same
kinds of stimuli.

This, we will argue, is not at all the kind of evolutionary logic that
Tomkins employs in his affect theory. While he is clearly indebted to
Darwin's phenomenology of discrete emotional responses (fear is different from anger, which is different from contempt), Tomkins's uses
for evolution are somewhat athwart the conventions (about biology,
about mind) that one will find in the work of Panksepp and his neo-
Darwinian contemporaries. We see Tomkins's approach to evolutionary data and his deployment of terms like *innate* as idiosyncratic and
less assimilable to an orthodox Darwinian lineage than many critical
commentators have assumed (see the interlude on Darwin). Indeed, his
enthusiasms for evolutionary theory provide a way for us to think about
affectivity other than through the intellectually exhausted and exhaust-
ing polemics of nature versus nurture, they map out conceptual territory
in which claims for universals in human psychology can be eschewed,
and they enable us to think about the dynamism rather than the stasis
of evolved biological systems.

We begin by suggesting that Tomkins is interested in evolutionary
theory to the extent that it can provide him with a conceptual infrastructure for thinking about how affects enter into combinatorial relations with each other and with other parts of mind. During his last

public lecture, in July 1990, Tomkins touched briefly on Darwin's evolutionary theories of emotion, and he clearly differentiated his own work on affect from that of Darwin. He noted, with particular emphasis, that Darwin took the face to be the site for the *expression* or *representation* of emotions, rather than, as Tomkins would like us to see, the site for the *production* of emotions (see chapter 2). Tomkins asserts that Darwin has an "archeological" understanding of the emotions: the face shows emotions that have originated elsewhere in the body, requiring Darwin to excavate for "[emotional] fossils and artifacts of the past" and bring them "to the surface." In contrast, Tomkins is seeking an **"inverse archeology"** of the affects, in which "the surface of the skin is where it's at, not deep within us." Put aphoristically, **"a smile is where it appears to be"** (*Exploring Affect,* 284). Here we see Tomkins's first point of departure from a conventional evolutionary account of mind. The affects do not emerge, fully formed, from buried substrata (those few ounces of subcortical tissue). They are not fossilized remnants of the past. Certainly the affects are neurological and phylogenetic for Tomkins, but not foundationally so; the affects are also always necessarily social, conscious, facial, scripted, ideological, and interpersonal. Tomkins is less interested in thinking of basic emotions (polished and specialized by millennia of human need) as the bedrock for affective life and much more interested in using phylogenetic or evolutionary data to think about an expansive, interconnected field of affective experience: **"if we want to understand feeling, we had better understand all the things that are conjoined and that have evolved to be conjoined"** (*Exploring Affect,* 285).

The status of "things that are conjoined" requires some elucidation, for it differs, in important ways, from the evolutionary ideal of adaptation in which, say, the cactus adapts to the dry conditions of the desert, a species of moth becomes more and more like the trees on which it lives, or (most famously) finches become differently modified to the ecology of their separate island homes. For Tomkins, things that have evolved to be conjoined aren't necessarily things that are well adapted ("no animal, of course, is completely adapted"; 1:27). If *conjoint* is one of Tomkins favorite adjectives, perhaps it is because the conditions of conjunction (and, we might add, disjunction) promise variance and friction much more than they promise consilience. He argues, for example, that natural selection has worked on man to "heighten three distinct classes of affect—affect for the preservation of life, affect for people and affect for novelty," yet "his integration of these needs cannot be perfect, nor can he be more than imperfectly adapted to his changing environment" (1:27). Here, then, is Tomkins's second important departure from the conventions of post-Darwinian evolutionary theory: while others might be entranced by the wonders of complementarity (think, for example, of the sublime fit of the hummingbird bill and a nectar-heavy flower), Tomkins is more compelled by the adulterated character of evolutionary outcomes. What is evolutionarily basic for Tomkins is not fitness but rather the capacity to conjoin and disjoin and cleave (see chapter 4).

In this sense, we see in Tomkins's use of evolutionary theory something similar to what Gillian Beer has elucidated in Darwin's work. Beer argues that "evolutionism has been so imaginatively powerful precisely because all its indications do not point one way. It is rich in contradictory elements. . . . Darwinian theory will not resolve to a single significance nor yield a single pattern. It is essentially multivalent" (*Darwin's Plots*, 6). The key, we maintain, to thinking about evolution in Tomkins's work is to think less in terms of foundations, syntheses, synchronies, and universals and more in the register of contingent amalgamations:

> Modern evolutionary theory portrays man as an adapted organism, fearfully and wonderfully made, but also imperfectly adapted because he is a patchwork thrown together, bit by bit, without a plan, remodeled opportunistically as occasions permitted. The conjoint operation of blind mutation, genetic recombination and natural selection contrived that magnificent makeshift, the human being. (1:24)

Conjoint, contrived, imperfect, makeshift. Evolution is deployed here to build a conceptual schema that can exemplify the interconnectedness of affects with each other and with cognitive, biological, social, and ideological systems: "**no affect is an island**" (3:216).

Three conceptual problematics emerge in thinking about Tomkins and evolution: (1) Are affects innate? (2) Are there phylogenetically basic emotions? (3) Are there universal (culturally invariant) affective responses? Let's take these questions one at a time. The innateness of the affects is one of the distinguishing characteristics of Tomkins's affect theory, and it has been noted by just about every commentator on his work. Here is Tomkins's most concise account of the innateness of the affects:

> Affects are sets of muscle and glandular responses located in the face and also widely distributed through the body, which generate sensory feedback which is either inherently "acceptable" or "unacceptable." These organized sets of responses are triggered at subcortical centers where specific "programs" for each distinct affect are stored. These programs are innately endowed and have been genetically inherited. They are capable when activated of simultaneously capturing such widely distributed organs as the face, the heart, and the endocrines and imposing on them a specific pattern of correlated responses. One does not learn to be afraid, or to cry, or to startle any more than one learns to feel pain or to gasp for air. (1:243–44)

At first blush, this may seem to be much the same account of the emotions that we saw in Panksepp: pregiven by phylogeny, present at birth, fixed in terms of their responsivity. Ruth Leys, for example, has been a vocal critic of Tomkins's work in this regard. Noting the influence of the evolutionary sciences on his affect theory, Leys argues that *innate* for Tomkins means universal, hardwired, reflex-like, noncognitive, and independent of learning.

We see something different in Tomkins's deployment of the term *innate*. The opening definition ("affects are sets of muscle and glandular responses") is subjected to significant elaboration as the chapter on the innate determinants of affect unfolds (a rhetorical trajectory typical in his writing). Crucially, the innate programs that are stored in subcortical centers are one component of a "complex" that encompasses other neurological events, the body's muscles, glands, organs, the face, consciousness, memory, motor signals, sensory messages, cognitive transformations, and learned behavioral responses. This multivalent assemblage is intensified by feedback, and it is mutable over time. Certainly Tomkins distinguishes between stored affect programs ("what is inherited as a subcortical structure which can instruct and control a variety of muscles and glands"; 1:244) and affect complexes, but he does not claim that innate affect programs monopolize or predetermine emotional life.

Indeed, in many places, Tomkins uses the term *affect* to apply equally to innate affect programs and to affect complexes, disrupting the inclinations we might have to order the affects according to conventional hierarchies of evolutionary or biological precedence.

Let's take the affect of fear as an example. Tomkins notes that while the innate stored program of fear has been "relatively invariant for some thousands of years" (3:502), the experience of fear is highly variable. One may experience fear in the face, the throat, the stomach, the genitals, the anus, or the heart or as a weakness in the knees, a dizziness in the head, or a trembling of the limbs (see our further elaboration of fear in chapter 6). That is, the innate components of the fear response have a contingent, rather than directly determining, relation to the fear that is felt. Importantly, the experiential variability that Tomkins describes here is not a supplemental event that modifies, in a fairly superficial way, a foundational neurological program (nature + a little nurture). Rather, he argues that innate affect programs are coextensive with all other activators (innate and learned), memories, images, messages, and percepts of the affect complex. No one part of this comprehensive systematicity can claim to be *the* element that underpins fear. In this way, Tomkins rewires one of the prime ideologies of neo-Darwinian evolutionary theory: he declines to use a phylogenetically inherited characteristic as a fixed point for, and determining cause of, psychological events—what Paul Ekman and Daniel Cordaro call "running the show" (366). In the end, for Tomkins, inherited affect programs are elements in, rather than the executive administrators of, affective life:

> Although there are affect activators which are quite independent of any learning or interpretive activity, no sooner do memory and analysis come into play than they too become activators of affect as potent as any of the inherited mechanisms. **Indeed, it is the inheritance of a flexible, varying central assembly structure capable of activating and combining affect with varying components of this assembly that, we propose, guarantees the basic freedom of the human being.** (1:248)

It follows from this idiosyncratic use of innate affect programs that Tomkins's affect theory fits poorly with some contemporary empirical literatures on basic emotions. In particular, we would like to argue, the claim that there is a coherent lineage of evolution-inclined theorists of basic emotion (Darwin–Tomkins–Ekman) has been overstated (we expand on this in the interlude on Darwin). While all three theorists argue for categorically distinct affects (fear is different from anger; joy is different from surprise), what is meant by "basic" emotions varies between these authors in ways that are conceptually and politically nontrivial. For example, in answer to the question "in what sense are basic emotions basic?" Ekman and Cordaro answer in orthodox terms:

> The basic emotions are discrete physiological responses to fundamental life situations that have been useful in our ancestral environment. These responses are universally shared within our species and some are also found in other primates. The basic emotions are not learned from our culture or environment, but rather they are prewired responses to a set of stimuli that have affected our species for tens of thousands of generations. (369)

Basic-ness, for Ekman, isn't just a measure of the discrete categorical differences between emotions; it is also an argument that emotions are biological in a fundamental, invariant way. In this sense, basic emotions are a weapon against the cultural relativism, linguisticism, and social constructionism that he feels brought the study of emotion into disrepute.

Tomkins is differently oriented toward the politics of affect theories. In the first instance, it is worth noting that Tomkins doesn't use the phrase "basic emotion." The phrase that he uses most is "primary affect," and it seems to us that in so doing, he is not only interested in the categorical and phylogenetic differences between some affective states; he is also keen to make visible the primacy of the affects as motivators of human behavior (see chapter 1). That is, the primary-ness of some affects refers, in part, to their elevated conceptual status in Tomkins's theory of mind. In this sense, Tomkins's "primary affects" do not just draw from evolution; they also push against the domination of drive-based and cognition-heavy theories of mind. If what is most conceptually and politically urgent for Ekman is advocating for basic emotions to censure cultural relativism and so consolidate a certain respectability for the study of emotion in psychology, what most galvanizes Tomkins is the capacity of the primary affects to remodel psychological theory from the ground up: "I continue to view affect as the primary biological motivating mechanism, more urgent than drive deprivation and pleasure and more urgent even than physical pain" (3:5). Carefully deployed, Tomkins's theory of primary affects promises a conceptual schema for thinking about psychological and evolutionary theory other than through the established creeds of biologism and social constructionism.

Ekman has also been a keen proponent of the thesis that the basic affects are *universal* (culturally invariant); they can be modified by display rules that are socially learned, but the core physiology of these emotions has been preset by phylogeny. An impassioned advocate for a certain mode of neo-Darwinian evolution, Ekman uses the universalism of emotional expression as an argument for the authority of biology (narrowly understood) to determine mental life. Again, we see significant differences between this kind of argument and the interests that Tomkins has in evolutionary data and the affects. While Tomkins agrees with Ekman that there is "overwhelming evidence of the universality of facial expression across cultures, among neonates, and even in the blind" (3:47), his target is not cultural relativism but cognitivism. Because Tomkins does not theorize the affects through biological or cognitive foundationalism, he does not use the idea of universal expression to consolidate the primacy of nature over nurture (or, indeed, the primacy of nurture over nature). Instead, and paradoxically, Tomkins uses the universality of facial expression to give affects a psychological distinctiveness that has been eliminated in a discipline that has increasingly come to regard cognition as king:

> The critical point is that the human being has evolved as a multimechanism system in which each mechanism is but one among many evokers of affect. Thinking can evoke feeling, but so can acting, so can perceiving, so can remembering, and so can one feeling evoke another feeling. It is this generality of evocation and coassembly which enables affect to serve for a system as complex and interdependent as the human being. (3:48)

This different trajectory in Tomkins's work becomes apparent in a number of places. For example, he is particularly interested in using phylogenetic and evolutionary data to build rich phenomenologies of differentiated and overlapping affective states. In a chapter on evolution and affect, Tomkins examines autonomic and endocrine data that illustrate the distinctive affective characteristics of animals that have been wrought by natural selection. As descriptions of adrenal and thyroidal differences unfold over many pages, it becomes clear that Tomkins has no heart for a traditional understanding of "the continuity of species" (Ekman, *Emotions Revealed,* 2); rather, he is most engaged by how evolutionary kinship generates affective *differences.* From a fairly simple, and potentially reductive, distinction between the adrenal glands and the thyroid, Tomkins builds what we might call "nonce" evolutionary taxonomies, where mismatches are as important as sleek adaptations of form and where systems of classification search not just for constancy but also for variance and discontinuity. The literary theorist Eve Kosofsky Sedgwick highlights the value of nonce taxonomies that evidence "the making and unmaking and *re*making and redissolution of hundreds of old and new categorical imaginings concerning all the kinds it may take to make up a world" (*Epistemology,* 23). The taxonomies of biological or phylogenetic worlds, we argue, are no less nonce-y, no less implicated in making, unmaking, and remaking, than the fictive worlds of Proust and James that Sedgwick engages.

FURTHER READING

Charles Darwin's *The Expression of the Emotions in Man and Animals* (1872) is his definitive engagement with emotion and evolution. We have drawn our account of Tomkins and evolution from chapter 5 ("Evolution and Affect") and chapter 8 ("The Innate Determinants of Affect") of *AIC1* and from his essay ("Affect Theory") in Paul Ekman's anthology *Emotion in the Human Face.* Tomkins's last public lecture, delivered at the International Society for Research on Emotion in 1990, has been published (in lightly edited form) as "Inverse Archaeology: Facial Affect and the Interfaces of Scripts within and between Persons" in *Exploring Affect: The Selected Writings of Silvan S. Tomkins.* This lecture is a long, often associative revision of his early work on affect and scripts. The arguments in this lecture are a summary of the findings in volumes 3 and 4 of *AIC.* Lauren Abramson has kindly shown us a video of this last lecture; our comments here draw from both the video and the published lecture.

We use the term consilience here and in chapter 13. It is a term that Edward O. Wilson popularized in a book of the same name in 1998 (*Consilience: The Unity of Knowledge*): "There is intrinsically only one class of explanation. It transverses the scales of space, time, and complexity to unite disparate facts of the disciplines by consilience, the perception of a seamless web of cause and effect" (297). A philosophy of consilience anticipates that the continuity of the world will eventually be reflected in one unbroken scientific account.

There is much to be said about Paul Ekman's long-standing battles with anthropological and psychological authors who reject biological or evolutionary explanations of emotion. We refer readers who would like to follow Ekman's side of this debate to his early text *Darwin and Facial Expression: A Century of Research in Review,* his afterword in Charles Darwin's *The Expression of the Emotions in Man and Animals,* and *Emotions Revealed: Recognizing Faces and Feelings to Improve Communication and Emotional Life.* His claims about the universal and hardwired nature of emotions and his rejection of theories of cultural relativism have remained much the same over the four decades covered by these texts.

4
FREEDOM

A contemporary reader of Tomkins may find it difficult to reconcile the posthumanist perspectives everywhere on offer in his writing with his blatant humanism. On one hand, we read an account of the human being as feedback mechanism and complex set of interdependent communication systems; on the other, we read bits of biblical exegesis and psychobiographies of the great Russian writers. Nowhere do these apparently contradictory discourses clash more resoundingly than in an early chapter of *AIC*, "Freedom of the Will and the Structure of the Affect System," where Tomkins routes the traditional philosophical problem of free will through "more recent developments in the theory of automata" (1:108). Presenting an elaborate thought experiment concerning the design of what we would now call cyborgs or androids, Tomkins develops a concept of affect freedom fundamentally defined in reference to machinic automaticity. In this chapter, we discuss his key idea of affect freedom and, along the way, offer some contexts for understanding the challenge it poses both to conventional humanist and contemporary posthumanist theory.

To begin, it is often helpful to remember that Tomkins was trained in philosophy. He received his doctorate from the University of Pennsylvania in 1934 with a thesis on eighteenth-century ethics ("Conscience, Self Love and Benevolence in the System of Bishop Butler," written under the supervision of Lewis Flaccus, a philosopher of aesthetics) before pursuing postdoctoral studies at Harvard with the logician W. V. O. Quine, among others. Tomkins moved from philosophy to psychology when he joined the Harvard Psychological Clinic under the directorship of Henry Murray (for more on Tomkins's work at Harvard, see chapter 11). This transition was not the marked disciplinary shift it would later become. So much early twentieth-century philosophy sought to resolve or dissolve traditional metaphysical problems using tools and techniques of the sciences. In this context, Tomkins's move to psychology should be understood as his adoption of a more thoroughgoing naturalistic account of the human. But even at its most empirical, his writing remains animated by speculative concerns and can best be thought of as a staging ground for encounters between philosophy, academic psychology, psychoanalysis, and the mid-century sciences of cybernetics and information theory.

Tomkins was particularly excited by the work of Norbert Wiener, whose *Cybernetics; or, Control and Communication in the Animal and the Machine* (1948) and *The Human Use of Human Beings: Cybernetics and Society* (1950) offered ideas that applied across disciplinary divides as well as ontological ones. Cybernetics appealed to Tomkins (and other thinkers) because it offered tools to translate metaphysical problems of human being into engineering ones. Specifically, it modeled purposive behavior without idealized notions of will or intention. Evelyn Fox Keller has located cybernetics as a consequence, in part, of "the intense concentration of technical efforts in World War II" from which there emerged "a science based on principles of feedback and circular causality, and aimed at the mechanical implementation of exactly the kind of purposive organization . . . that was so vividly exemplified by biological organisms" (65). She points out that what had been, in the previous century, a productive analogy between biological and mechanical self-regulation became in Wiener's work a homology or even an identity. Machines and animals enter a new, and highly charged, deconstructive relation, with the mid-century sciences of organized complexity exerting strong pressure on the category of the human and prompting scientists to pose questions like, How can we model human behavior and experience in terms of feedback relations between complex systems? What kind of machine, or aggregate of machines, is the human being? (See chapter 12 for more on cybernetics.)

Like that of other cyberneticians, Tomkins's thinking is characterized by a strong commitment to complexity. Consider how he begins his discussion of the "pseudo problem of the freedom of the will" by tackling "the conventional concept of causality, which . . . assumed that the relationship between events was essentially two-valued, either determinate or capricious, and that man's will was therefore either slavishly determined or capriciously free" (1:109). Turning away from this notion of linear causality associated with eighteenth-century mechanism, Tomkins introduces the "complexity or degrees-of-freedom principle," a formal concept based on statistical mechanics: "By complexity, we mean, after Gibbs, the number of independently variable states of a system" (1:110). In the second, revised edition of *The Human Use of Human Beings* (1954), Wiener frames the contributions of cybernetics by way of the work of Willard Gibbs and "the impact of the Gibbsian point of view on modern life" (11). A nineteenth-century U.S. mathematician and physicist, Gibbs developed influential mathematical treatments of the laws of thermodynamics that would be taken up by Claude Shannon in his theory of communication. Gibbs also worked on the mathematization of particle distributions, permitting more adequate representations of an observer's contingent and uncertain (i.e., probabilistic) knowledge. The "Gibbsian point of view," then, contrasts with the Laplacian worldview in which an observer can, in principle, predict outcomes based on certain knowledge of initial conditions.

Rather than argue against causality or determination as such (as do many voices in contemporary posthumanist theory), Tomkins turns to statistical mechanics to dislink questions of determination from those of freedom: **"Two systems may be equally determined, but one . . . more free than the other"** (1:110). Of "two chess programs, the one which considers more possibilities before it decides on each move is the freer general strategy" (1:110). In Tomkins's redefinition, freedom becomes an index to the complexity of a system, that is, to the range and variety of possible responses to environmental conditions. While each of these responses is itself determined, it is not necessarily predictable (a consequence of the complexity of the system). The tools of information theory permit Tomkins to pluralize and to relativize the traditional philosophical dilemma ("The problem of free will can be translated into the problem of the relative degrees of freedom of the human being" [1:110]) and to operationalize the notion of freedom. He proposes to measure the freedom of any given feedback system in terms of "the product of the complexity of its 'aims' and the frequency of their attainment" (1:110) and concludes that "a human being thus becomes freer as his wants grow and as his capacities to satisfy them grow. Restriction either of his wants or abilities to achieve them represents a loss of freedom" (1:111).

Philosophically, Tomkins's understanding of freedom in terms of expanded capacities resembles Spinoza's writing in the *Ethics* on affect and the capacity for action (see our first interlude). At the same time, it is difficult not to hear Tomkins's discussion in its sociopolitical context as an American response to postwar existentialism and the global expansion of consumerism. (It is interesting to note how his writing in the 1970s and 1980s offers alternatives to his earlier emphasis on what he calls the "mini-maximizing strategies of power" [3:243] that underlie this earlier notion of freedom.) Tomkins's liberal-sounding humanism may be one reason why his writing continues to be difficult to access in a contemporary theoretical scene that often rejects perceived liberalisms. While it would be easy to assimilate his politics with Wiener's, who tended to oscillate between extremes of optimism and pessimism in promoting a technocratic, cybernetic vision of both self and society, in fact Tomkins was much less worried about the coherence and autonomy of self and less committed to totalizing theories of society. His theory of value is open ended and pluralist to the extreme ("It is our theory of value that for human subjects value is any object of human affect" [1:329]). As a consequence, his humanism is capacious rather than prescriptive, exemplary of a scientific humanism that accepts the species designation for descriptive and investigative purposes.

It is his emphatic insistence on the crucial role for affect in understanding freedom that defines Tomkins's approach to human being:

> The human being is the most complex system in nature; his superiority over other animals is as much a consequence of his more complex affect system as it is of his more complex analytical capacities. Out of the marriage of reason with affect there issues clarity with passion. **Reason without affect would be impotent, affect without reason would be blind.** The combination of affect and reason guarantees man's high degree of freedom. (1:112)

We will return to Tomkins's understanding of the relation between affect and cognition in our last chapter (chapter 14). It is one of his most significant, and least understood, contributions. Far from being seamlessly integrated with cognition, the initial independence of the affect system from other elements of the feedback system accounts for its role in expanding capacities for action. His argument concerns the relation between the affect system and the "transmuting mechanism" that defines consciousness (see chapter 7). Recall that, according to Tomkins, the infant's distress, anger, and other affects are general motives that do not lead the infant to take any specific, goal-oriented actions. By contrast with the drives, which involve programs that are instrumentally connected to the human feedback system (for example, the infant's hunger triggers salivation and sucking), the affects "will remain independent of the feedback system until the infant discovers that something can be done about such vital matters" (1:113). This independence means that "most human beings never attain great precision of control of their affects" (1:114). It is the "ambiguity and blindness" (1:114) of the affect system, a consequence of its "imperfect integration" (1:114) into the human being's feedback system, that paradoxically secures greater degrees of freedom by creating possibilities for learning.

Tomkins's fundamental point concerns mistake, both cognitive and motivational: "Cognitive strides are limited by the motives which urge them. Cognitive error, which is essential to cognitive learning, can be made only by one capable of committing motivational error, i.e. being wrong about his own wishes, their causes and outcomes" (1:114). Once again, Tomkins recasts psychoanalytic ideas (here repetition compulsion) in cybernetic terms: "the residues of past human learning, our habits, are essentially stored neurological programs which may be run off with a minimum of learning" (1:114). Human beings (and, presumably, other animals) automatize what has been learned. At the same time that this permits them to adapt to changing environmental conditions, it interferes with the ability to change:

> Part of the power of the human organism and its adaptability lies in the fact that in addition to innate neurological programs the human being has the capacity to lay down new programs of great complexity on the basis of risk taking, error and achievement—programs designed to deal with contingencies not necessarily universally valid but valid for his individual life. This capacity to make automatic or nearly automatic what was once voluntary, conscious and learned frees consciousness, or the transmuting mechanism, for new learning. But just as the freedom to learn involves freedom for cognitive

and motivational error, so the ability to develop new neurological programs, that is, the ability to use what was learned with little or no conscious monitoring, involves the ability to automatize, and make unavailable to consciousness, both errors and contingencies which were once appropriate but which are no longer appropriate. (1:114–15)

It can be difficult to alter old habits precisely because they once worked so well. This is as true of an idiosyncratic piano technique as of the patterns of our loves. "The essential quality of man as we see it is not in the amount of information he possesses but in the mechanism which enables him constantly to increase his freedom" (1:115), and yet the same automatizing mechanism that increases our capacity for action by permitting us to adapt to an environment also interferes with our ability to perceive and respond to a new one. Thus, for Tomkins, human freedom is defined in terms of an automaticity that everywhere both enables and undermines it.

Tomkins's commitment to understanding human automaticity emerges most clearly in an elaborate thought experiment on "the design of human-like automata" (1:115). Unlike the ideally rational chess-playing machines of the nascent mid-century field of artificial intelligence, Tomkins sought to imagine a full-blooded automaton that "would represent not the disembodied intelligence of an auxiliary brain but a mechanical intelligence intimately wed to the automaton's own complex purposes" (1:119), a cyborg that resembes those in Philip K. Dick's *Do Androids Dream of Electric Sheep?* (1968). There would be much to say about Tomkins's entertaining, maternal alternative to conventional AI, ranging from his criticism of the automaton designer as "an overprotective, overdemanding parent who is too pleased with precocity in his creations" (1:116) to his fantasy of how humanlike automata would reproduce and create societies. For our purposes, we would briefly point to the crucial place of the affect system in these automata: "there must be built into such a machine a number of responses which have selfrewarding and self-punishing characteristics. . . . These are essentially aesthetic characteristics of the affective responses" (1:117). Tomkins insists that these aesthetic qualities not be defined "in terms of the immediate behavioral responses to it, since it is the gap between these affective responses and instrumental responses which is necessary if it is to function like a human motivational response" (1:118). There are a number of significant gaps in this automaton's affect system: "There must be introduced into the machine a critical gap between the conditions which instigate the self-rewarding or self-punishing responses, which maintain them and which turn them off, and the 'knowledge' of these conditions and the further response to the knowledge of these conditions" (1:118). These various gaps (between the conditions of affect activation/ maintenance/deactivation, the automaton's awareness of these conditions, and its ability to respond once it has become aware) create considerable play in the feedback system as a whole, making it possible for the automaton to make mistakes and to learn. These gaps, at once conjunctive and disjunctive, are conditions for the generality of affect and the particular freedoms of the affect system. (For a discussion of Tomkins's emphasis on gaps in relation to evolution, see chapter 3.)

We have been selectively summarizing the first half of a long chapter from *AIC1*, the second half of which consists of a discussion of the varieties of freedom in the affect system, including freedoms of time, intensity, and density; freedom of object; freedom of coassembly; freedom of consummatory site; and others. We find particularly fruitful those of Tomkins's ideas that seek to update the early grounding of psychoanalysis in nineteenth-century thermodynamics by way of the mid-twentieth-century sciences of cybernetics and information theory. For example, he suggests that whereas the drives function primarily via homeostatic mechanisms that regulate internal environments, "the affect system of man operates . . . within a much more uncertain and variable environment" (1:124) characterized by an abundance of information. He offers several emendations of classical psychoanalysis, proposing that "had Freud not smuggled some of the properties of the affect system into his conception of the drives, his system would have been of much less interest than it was" (1:127). Gesturing toward a revision of the theory of sexual development (the oral, anal, and genital stages), he states that Freud's emphasis on the sexuality of the oedipus complex "obscured the significance of the family romance as an expression of the more general wishes to be both the mother and father, and to possess both of them, quite apart from the fear which might be generated by a jealous sexual rival" (1:127). Tomkins's basic point about the transformability of the affects ("**it is** the affects, not the drives, which are transformable" [1:143]) is part of a reconsideration of sublimation (1:141–43). Most of these emendations are consequences of Tomkins's emphatic commitment to the freedom of object: "There is literally no kind of object which has not historically been linked to one or another of the affects" (1:133). His discussion of "affect–object reciprocity" (1:133–35) explores phenomena that psychoanalysis describes in terms of the defenses of projection and introjection; here he proposes that the "somewhat fluid relationship between affects and their objects" (1:134) is necessary for knowledge projects of all kinds.

It is fitting that this chapter on the freedom of the affect system ends with a discussion of the restrictions on freedom inherent in the affect system. Tomkins notes that affective responses seem, phenomenologically, to be "the primitive gods within the individual" (1:144) over which humans have little control. He describes this lack of control in information theoretical terms of high redundancy ("If one end of the continuum of complexity is freedom of choice of alternatives, then the other end is redundancy" [1:143]) and speculates about the sources of this high redundancy. These include the evolutionary relation between the affects and the primary drive deficit states (1:144–45), the "syndrome characteristic" of affect (the innervation of all parts at once in affective response; 1:146), the contagion of affect (affect arousal itself arouses more affect; 1:146), and other redundancies. Tomkins's goal is to sketch a model of the human being that leads to a realistic assessment of how persons can change. But this model is not static: because the conditions for change themselves change, and because humans are so complex, it is impossible to predict how or when conditions may alter, leading to fundamental shifts in relation to freedom. Tomkins's commitment to automaticity, then, is everywhere accompanied by a commitment to the biological contingency of the human animal. These are exemplary of his scientific humanism.

FURTHER READING

Our discussion is largely based on "Freedom of the Will and the Structure of the Affect System" (chapter 4 of *AIC1*). We also consulted some scholarship on cybernetics. For more on the complex category self-organization, see Evelyn Fox Keller's "Organisms, Machines, and

Thunderstorms: A History of Self-Organization, Part One." On Norbert
Wiener and mid-century liberal subjectivity, see N. Katherine Hayles's
"Liberal Subjectivity Imperiled: Norbert Wiener and Cybernetic Anxi-
ety" in *How We Became Posthuman* (1999). On the relations between
cybernetics and deconstruction, see Christopher Johnson's *System and
Writing in the Philosophy of Jacques Derrida* (1993), and for more on
Tomkins's involvement in the computer simulation of personality, and
its broader relations to research in the field of artificial intelligence, see
Elizabeth A. Wilson's *Affect and Artificial Intelligence* (2010).

For a detailed clinical case history of the affective dynamics involved
in the repetition compulsion, see Virginia Demos's *The Affect Theory of
Silvan Tomkins for Psychoanalysis and Psychotherapy* (chapter 7).

Degrees of freedom *(d.f.)* is a formal statistical calculation commonly used in psychology experiments to represent how much variance
there is in a data set. A larger data set has more degrees of freedom than
a smaller data set. Tomkins is using the term to indicate how complexity varies in different systems: some systems (e.g., human beings) have
more degrees of freedom (more opportunities for variation) than other
systems (e.g., amoebas).

5
THE POSITIVE

So far we have been exploring those aspects of Tomkins's writing that address the affect system in general (in relation to the drives, to the face, to evolution, and to freedom). In this chapter and the next, we turn to his exploration of the individual affects. Much of the interest and enjoyment we take in reading *AIC* comes from Tomkins's persuasive descriptions of specific feelings and our at times startling encounters with ourselves and others in these psychodynamic accounts. The rapid movement in his writing between fine-grained phenomenology (a kind of close reading) and bold theoretical generalization leads to the unusual sense of a loosely integrated, systemic understanding of subjectivity: dynamic, complex, open, but nevertheless coherent.

This is not to say that Tomkins is always convincing. In these chapters, we leave aside contentious questions concerning the existence, specification, and proper naming of the affects, debates ongoing today as they were in the early 1960s. We also leave aside substantive discussion of Tomkins's model of innate activation, which proposes that the affects are activated by different gradients of the "density of neural firing" over time (1:251). This model has not, to our knowledge, been empirically tested. Indeed, given Tomkins's refusal to speculate about brain localization (where would such neural firing take place, exactly?), it is not clear how such a test could be devised. But whatever its empirical status, this model is good to think with. "The general advantage of affective arousal to such a broad spectrum of levels and changes of level of neural firing is to make the individual care about quite different states of affairs in different ways" (1:252): because an affect can be activated by any "state of affairs" that matches its activation profile (for example, startle by any sufficiently steep positive gradient, internal or external, whether a gunshot, a tap on the shoulder, or a new idea), affective qualities play constitutive roles in an enormous variety of psychic experience. We

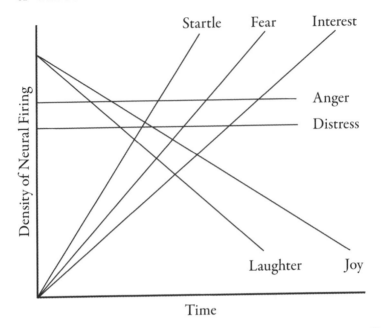

Graphical representation of a theory of innate activators of affect. From *Affect Imagery Consciousness,* 1:251.

consider some such model, at once specific and general, particularizing and abstracting, to be necessary for developing an adequate understanding of affect.

The first affect to which Tomkins turns, and the one he considers to be the "most seriously neglected" (1:337), is interest-excitement. Interest does not appear in most catalogs of emotion. It is absent, for example, from Darwin's study, a fact that Tomkins explains this way: Darwin "misidentified the affect [of interest-excitement] with the function of thinking" (1:337–38). Because of the phenomenon of psychic fusion (see chapter 2), it can be difficult to distinguish interest from the experiences that it often accompanies and amplifies, including perception and thinking, but also sexual arousal, surprise, and the orientation reflexes. Locating interest-excitement in, but also distinguishing it from, these other experiences lets Tomkins focus on its specifically positive quality, that is, its capacity to motivate. It is because interest-excitement is so rewarding that it can play many roles for the human being: as "a support of the necessary and the possible" (1:342), as "a necessary condition for the formation of the perceptual world" (1:347) and in creative experiences of all kinds, and as a crucial element in what Tomkins will call commitment scripts. We will briefly discuss each of these roles for interest.

First, it may be helpful to consider how Tomkins distinguishes interest-excitement (and its characteristic facial expression: eyebrows down, track, look, listen) from surprise-startle (eyebrows up, mouth open, eye blink). He calls surprise "the resetting affect" and describes it as neutral or somewhat negative in quality, depending on its intensity. For Tomkins, "**the salient characteristic of the startle mechanism— its capacity for interruption of any ongoing activity**" (1:499), gives it the role of "a circuit breaker": "This mechanism is similar in design and function to that in a radio or television network which enables special announcements to interrupt any ongoing program" (1:498). Surprise-startle has the function of clearing the central assembly to prepare for a subsequent central assembly that takes into account the information that activated the surprise response in the first place (for more on the central assembly, see chapter 12). By contrast, the function of interest-excitement, which is activated by *"optimal rates of increase of stimulation density"* (1:341) (a positive gradient that is not as steep as either surprise or fear), is "to 'interest' the human being in what is *necessary* and what is *possible* for him to be interested in" (1:342). While surprise breaks existing circuits, interest extends them, creates new connections, and expands our experiential networks.

To clarify this point, Tomkins considers the consequences of the utter absence of interest in, say, a depressive who is unable to motivate himself or herself to get out of bed or a domesticated cat who, "once it has thoroughly explored its environment . . . loses its characteristic curiosity and spends much of its adult life sleeping" (1:343). Interest motivates wakefulness, perception, and cognition to the point that "**absence of the affective support of interest would jeopardize intellectual development no less than destruction of brain tissue**" (1:343). Because of its crucial role in a variety of "sub-systems—the drives, perceptual, cognitive, and motoric apparatuses, as well as their organization into central assemblies, and governing Images" (1:344), interest-excitement supports both what is necessary for existence (the development of motor skills necessary for eating, say) and what is possible (learning to ride a bicycle or create new forms of warfare). And just as intense excitement can produce insomnia, so can this rewarding affect have destructive consequences: "The realm of the possible is equally the realm of the wonderful, the trivial, the distressing and the terrifying. Excitement enables an enrichment of life in ways which may or may not enhance what is necessary for existence. In the extremity, the quest for excitement may destroy the individual" (1:345).

Because excitement is the only positive affective response to novelty (surprise and fear, also responses to novelty, are not positive), it plays a key role in perception and creativity. "All animals are much more creative than they are credited" (1:353), suggests Tomkins, whose broad understanding of "creative perception, thought, and action" (1:353) includes sexual exploration, intellectual activity, and learning ability. Early in human development, interest-excitement plays a key role in motivating the many forms of acquaintance (perceptual, conceptual, motor, and memory) necessary for the infant to achieve basic competence with whole objects (1:348–49). Acknowledging that not everyone pursues sustained creative activities after childhood, Tomkins discusses the affective conditions both for "the deceleration of creativity as the adult develops" (1:353–54) and for the development of what he calls "an addiction to thinking" (1:357) and "an inner life" (1:358). This latter topic was of special interest to Tomkins, who consistently illustrates his theoretical writing with case studies of exemplary thinkers, writers, artists, performers, and activists. For example, his paper "The Psychology of Commitment" examines four nineteenth-century abolitionist reformers and their dedication to the antislavery movement in the United States to argue both for the predominant role of interest-excitement in what he terms commitment scripts and for the crucial role of alternating positive and negative affects and the place of violence and suffering in reforming democratic societies. In his chapter on excitement in *AIC*, his primary example of a commitment script is Freud. Here, once again, Tomkins emphasizes the role of both negative and positive affects in the development of "radical intellectual creativity," listing various "ingredients" in what amounts to an unfollowable recipe for the making of a personality such as Freud's.

"I am, above all, what excites me" (1:347): according to Tomkins, excitement is the affect most implicated in the many different kinds of personalities and senses of self. Enjoyment-joy, on the other hand, contributes most fundamentally to recognition of others and the social bond. While distinct, these positive affects necessarily enter into complex reciprocal relation. Consider, for example, that at the same time that interest-excitement, as a response to novelty, motivates the infant's exploration of objects in its world, enjoyment-joy helps the infant experience these objects as familiar by "providing some containment" (1:488) for perception. "A familiar object is not only recognized but it is kept in awareness longer" (1:489): enjoyment motivates the return to an object that is now both exciting and enjoyable. At later stages of development, such reciprocal interaction between the positive affects can create what Tomkins calls addictions (1:493–97). His writings on addiction and commitment, in the first volume of *AIC* and elsewhere, are precursors to the more general idea of script theory that Tomkins develops in the 1970s (see chapter 9).

While much psychological literature argues that the smile response is innately released by the sight of the human face, Tomkins argues that the smile (the characteristic facial expression of enjoyment-joy) is "innately activated by any relatively steep reduction of the density of stimulation of neural firing" (1:371). The smile of enjoyment, or its more intense form, the laugh, may be activated by a variety of steep reductions, for example, of other affects: a sudden reduction of distress or fear may produce the smile of relief, a sudden reduction of anger may produce the laugh of triumph, a sudden reduction of excitement the smile of recognition. (Characteristically, for Tomkins, relief, triumph, and recognition are distinct emotions that share the affect of enjoyment-joy at their core.) As we have shown (see chapter 3), Tomkins does not reject an evolutionary perspective but offers a larger, more systemic, and less strictly adaptationist framework in which to account for the smile's significance: "Man is one of those animals whose individual survival and group reproduction rests heavily on social responsiveness and the mutual enjoyment of each other's presence is one of the most important ways in which social interaction is rewarded and perpetuated" (1:399). In his analysis, the rewards of enjoyment-joy are mutual and resemble those of sexual intercourse; unlike sex, however, enjoyment "operates at a distance rather than requiring body contact" (1:397). Falling in love, as Tomkins points out, is often accompanied by powerfully mutual experiences of staring and smiling, a *felicité a deux* that evokes the mother–infant dyad.

This dyad serves as a template for later social communion. Building on Harry Harlow's famous rhesus monkey experiments (in which baby monkeys prefer to cling to a surrogate mother covered with terry cloth, even when they had the option of a wire and wood surrogate that provided food), Tomkins suggests that, for humans, smiling replaces clinging as the primary bond between infant and mother. While he does not underestimate the role of bodily contact in infancy ("The body of the mother, of course, becomes the focus of a complex affect and drive matrix" [1:406]), he proposes that it is the distance permitted by the smile response that radically expands the capacities for human communion. Here Tomkins demonstrates both his indebtedness to classical psychoanalytic thinking and a strong need to find less reductive ways to express its major insights. "The equation of oral interests with every type of human dependence and interdependence has masked the critical role both of the face and of the distance receptors in human communion" (1:407), suggests Tomkins, who offers distinctly non-Freudian understandings of development. For example, rather than the drama of sexual development and progression through (oral, anal, and genital) stages, Tomkins proposes that "if early modes of communion are enjoyed side by side with later modes, we regard this as the true normal development. We do not regard these early modes either as exclusively infantile nor perverse" (1:418). Here is one of Tomkins's more explicit critiques of Freudianism: "Implicit in his theory is a hidden value judgment that early communion is helpless, dependent, greedy and blind to the separateness of the love object, and as such to be transcended in development and to be perverse if it is not" (1:421).

What emerges most clearly in these pages on enjoyment-joy is Tomkins's refusal to pathologize communion and dependency. He offers a broad appreciation of communion at a historical moment in postwar America when this idea was most often perceived as a threat to individual autonomy in terms of a dangerous absorption into ideological, familial, or maternal groups (Communism, McCarthyism, groupthink, the organization man, momism, and so on). His formal technique for depathologizing the enjoyment of communion is the written list. Hosts of examples are adduced under headings like "Types of Mutual

Shared Enjoyments," "Types of Complementary Enjoyments," "Types of Mismatches of Identical Social Needs," "Types of Mismatches of Social Needs Based on the Inability to Initiate Communion," and "Conflicts Produced by the Diversity of Social Needs." Some of these ways of enjoying and failing to enjoy one another include **"If you enjoy being hugged and I enjoy hugging you, it can be mutually enjoyable. If you enjoy being dominated and I enjoy controlling you, we may enjoy each other"** (1:412); "If you would like to share your ideas with me and I would like to share my ideas with you but neither of us can communicate in such a way until the other has initiated it, we may never come to understand each other" (1:413); "You wish to reveal yourself through your view of the nature of man, but I can externalize myself only through communicating my passion for the steel and tape of a computer that almost thinks like a man" (1:414). The cumulative effect of these lists (and lists of lists) is to transform moral hierarchies into affective matches and mismatches, leveling the playing field of value.

Instead of hierarchy, we get a grand survey of modes of communion, beginning with those preverbal modes based on early scenes of infant feeding that "exert a powerful hold on the minds and bodies of all human beings" (1:419). Not only does Tomkins discuss thumb sucking, smoking, and eating and drinking as cognates of the early scene of the baby at the breast, he also discusses claustral experiences more generally. Underwater skin diving, immersive music, interocular intimacy, "the cloistered halls of the university" (1:419), "the enjoyment of silent, smooth-riding automobiles" (1:423), these and many others are occasions for "a continuing enjoyment of the earliest modes of communion affect, unverbalized and unrecognized as such" (1:426). In the context of modernist critical traditions that valorize the shattering effects of *jouissance* and the pleasures of transgression, it can be a relief simply to be reminded of a set of quieter enjoyments that may exist alongside "the breaking through of enforced restraint" (1:422) associated with excitement and novelty. A valuable aspect of Tomkins's theory, we think, is that neither excitement nor enjoyment (nor any of the affects) has any exclusive political or ideological valence as such. Political valences quickly emerge, however, with the inevitable embedding of affects in scenes and scripts that connect them to specific objects, situations, ideas, and behaviors. The affects themselves can become objects and agents of ideology, for example, in scripts that gender them or cluster them in historical relations between oppressors and oppressed (we will return to the subject of ideology in chapters 10 and 13).

Tomkins also addresses speech as a mode of communion. Here he offers a distinctly non-Lacanian account of language acquisition, not in terms of the violent and irrevocable loss of the maternal object as the condition of entrance into the Symbolic, but almost the opposite: "The major motive to speech is, paradoxically, the intensely rewarding claustral and pre-verbal social affect" (1:428). The ideas in these pages may strike some readers in the theoretical humanities as naive or sentimental: "Earliest speech is an attempt to commune, to deepen experienced communion rather than an attempt to communicate, in the sense of expressing a personal message to the other. . . . Its aim is essentially no different than a tightening and clinging to the mother, by an infant who is already clinging" (1:429). But the umbrella idea of speech as communion permits Tomkins to embrace a large variety of functions for speech, both cognitive (the communication of information) and affective ("as an instrument for the evocation or reduction of every kind of affect, in the self or in others" [1:430]). If speech, for adults, serves as "a major vehicle of the expression of his affects" (1:442), this vehicle will sometimes attenuate those affects that would otherwise be inhibited and amplify those that would otherwise subside. And what psychologists call "expression" is by no means the whole story: in "art and ideology . . . affects can be extraordinarily modulated and amplified, enriched and deepened. Imagination, aided by words, has created worlds which have completely captured the minds of men, evoking and creating rather than expressing affects, and binding the evoked affects to possibilities which are eventually actualized just because men were inspired to dream and then to act" (1:443). Tomkins begins to sketch a complex performative account of *poesis* ("creating rather than expressing," as he puts it) in which speech and writing evoke affect that can motivate both further representation (dream) and action.

We have no room here to go into any detail, even the most summary, concerning Tomkins's discussions of identification as a source of communion, the interesting emergence in these pages of what he calls the depressive posture, or the ways that enjoyment competes with other positive affect (the excitement of novelty) or with negative affect ("**The general role of enjoyment is critical in promoting courage to cope with fear and pain, and in promoting frustration tolerance**" [1:478]). It may be appropriate simply to leave the reader with a list of section titles under the main title "Adult Modes of Communion," a list that we hope will evoke the characteristic range and texture of Tomkins's ideas: "Doing for Others as a Mode of Communion," "Doing Things Together as a Mode of Communion," "Controlling Others as a Mode of Communion," "Doing Things before Others as a Mode of Communion," "Drive Satisfaction as a Mode of Communion," "The Enjoyment of the Expression of Negative Affects as a Mode of Communion," and finally, "The Attenuation of Communion as a Mode of Communion."

FURTHER READING

Our discussion is largely based on several chapters from *AIC1*: "Interest-Excitement" (chapter 10), "Enjoyment-Joy and the Smiling Response: Developmental, Physiological, and Comparative Aspects" (chapter 11), "The Dynamics of Enjoyment-Joy: The Social Bond" (chapter 12), and "Surprise-Startle: The Resetting Affect" (chapter 13). We also consulted his essays on commitment scripts and addiction: "The Psychology of Commitment. Part 1: The Constructive Role of Violence and Suffering for the Individual and for His Society" (1965), "Psychological Model of Smoking Behavior" (1966), "A Modified Model of Smoking Behavior" (1968), "Some Varieties of Psychological Organization" (1968), and, with Frederick Ikard, "The Experience of Affect as a Determinant of Smoking Behavior" (1973).

On the topic of affect nomenclature, Tomkins writes, "Although consensus on the number and nature of the primary affects has not yet been attained and although there is also considerable variation concerning the proper names for each affect, we will nonetheless attempt . . . tentatively to standardize the terminology of affect in the hope that this may lead to more research, subsequent consensus and an eventual more valid description and nomenclature" (1:336). His nomenclature did effectively lead to more research (by Ekman and many others), and there is some consensus today among those who support the existence of four or five so-called basic emotions. Lisa Feldman Barrett offers a significant dissenting voice on this issue in the psychology of emotion. We also note that Daniel Stern takes up and modifies Tomkins's model in a discussion of the "vitality affects" in *The Interpersonal World of the Infant* (1985).

6
THE NEGATIVE

The negative affects take up a lot of space in Tomkins's affect theory. The second volume of *AIC* opens with the cry of distress-anguish and is then occupied for more than four hundred pages with the vicissitudes of shame-humiliation and contempt-disgust. The third volume, published almost thirty years later, follows the fortunes of anger-rage and fear-terror. In all, twenty-five chapters across two volumes describe the sources, scripting, and socialization of these primary negative affects.

Why do the negative affects occupy so much of Tomkins's attention? This question has a number of answers, but they all begin with Tomkins's disarmingly concise characterization of the negative affects as *inherently unacceptable.* That is, the affects of shame, anger, fear, contempt, distress, disgust, and dissmell are experienced as punitive (**"All the negative affects trouble human beings deeply. Indeed, they have evolved just to amplify and deepen suffering and to add insult to the injuries of the human condition"** [3:111]), and the noxiousness of these affective states is direct and immediate ("One does not learn to be afraid, or to cry, or to startle any more than one learns to feel pain or to gasp for air" [1:244]). How to deal with the toxicity of these affects is a significant problem for the individual and for the environments in which those individuals dwell (the home, the office, the hospital, the schoolyard, the street, or the factory, to name some of the settings that Tomkins argues can become saturated in negative affect). The negative affects are an inescapable problem that requires considerable psychological and social engagement. In principle, all of the negative affects can be down-regulated; in practice, how successful each one of us—or a group of us together—can be in effectively managing negative affect remains an open question. My anger may be quiescent today, but next week it may be amplified to levels of fury that I can no longer adequately manage; you may join me in this righteous anger, helping me down-regulate the toxicity of my rage, and we may form a lifelong alliance against the object that has provoked us, or my anger may now be so bitter as to make any bond between us impossible.

As we have noted in previous chapters, Tomkins's claim that the affects are activated by innate physiological mechanisms can cause some discomfort in critical environments that are accustomed to giving causal priority to social or significatory or discursive forces. His claim that the primary affects are activated by "density of neural firing" might also be met with disbelief, disdain, or just plain exhaustion by those critics increasingly uncomfortable with the slick ways in which neurological data are mobilized inside the humanities or social sciences as palliatives to interpretation, ambivalence, or uncertainty. To these discomforts, we add two more: the negative affects cannot be repurposed as good feeling, nor are they reliable agents for political transformation. While the negative affects may be down-regulated, or suppressed, or put into reciprocal relations with the positive affects, or modulated through socialization (more of which below), at no point do they lose their noxious character, and they remain a source of significant trouble psychologically, interpersonally, and socially. On this point Tomkins is clear: **"negative affect should be minimized"** (1:328). Human beings are strongly motivated to avoid or minimize negative affects, and the extent to which affective negativity can be harnessed to affirmative ends like social justice, world building, or conceptual clarity will always be limited. For example, anger (an affect central to struggles for political transformation) seems to be a particularly unruly kind of negativity:

> Terror speaks to the threat of death to life. Distress is the affect of suffering, making of the world a vale of tears. Shame is the affect of indignity, of defeat, of transgression, and of alienation, striking deep into the heart of the human being and felt as an inner torment, a sickness of the soul. But anger is problematic above all other negative affects for its social consequences. My terror, my distress, and my shame are first of all my problems. They *need* never become your problems, though they may. But my anger, and especially my rage, threatens violence for you, your family, your friends, and above all for our society. Of all the negative affects it is the least likely to remain under the skin of the one who feels it, and so it is just that

affect all societies try hardest to contain within that envelope under the skin or to deflect toward deviants within the society and toward barbarians without. (3:111)

The enduring social and political problem is not simply that deviants and barbarians may be subjected to the punitive effects of displaced anger but that anger will produce social effects that confound all parties, including those that take an ethical, angry stand against social discrimination. That is, there is no firm distinction between anger that emancipates and anger that is deflected into social control, violation, or harm. You, me, them, and our social worlds will all be shaken by an angry negativity that has breached the surface of the skin. Anger "makes bad matters worse" (2:115), and that is the power and the threat of its political purchase. As we describe the ways in which negative affects combine with other affects and how they come to be socialized and minimized, we would like the reader to remember that these are not accounts of abstinence from negativity or accounts of negativity bending to the good but rather descriptions of how negative affects come to be more or less tolerable.

There are six primary negative affects in Tomkins's theory. Here we summarize their distinguishing characteristics.

Distress-anguish. Imagine a desolate, crying baby. Her mouth is open, yet the corners of her lips are pulled down, her eyebrows are arched, and the muscles around her eyes are contracted. For Tomkins, these facial states don't express negative feeling that has originated elsewhere in the body; rather, the awareness of the feedback from these physiological events *is* the feeling of distress. These facial responses and the distressing feeling they engender are caused by a high level of unrelenting stimulation: the baby is pained, cold, overheated, hungry, alarmed by intense noise or light. While distress is innately activated by such circumstances, the phenomenological experience of distress varies widely as the feedback assembles with different cognitive information and with other affects. Consequently, we may learn, through socialization, to become distressed about a large number of objects: "the possible objects of distress are limited only by the imagination of the parent who cares enough to make the child distressed about whatever it is which he wishes to discourage in the child. Clearly this usually encompasses the control of behavior and belief as well as the control of affects. Historically, at some time or place, every variety of behavior has been made the object of suffering. Parents have made it distressing to be overly active or passive, to be bold or cautious, or to be overly friendly or too reserved" (2:52). While an adult may be readily distressed by certain memories, persons, or objects, it is rare to see the full cry of distress in an adult: "It is a brief cry, or a muted cry, or a part of a cry or a miniature cry, or a substitute cry, or an active defense against the cry, that we see in place of the infant's cry for help" (2:56). Finally, we note that there is a particularly close relation between distress-anguish and the positive affect interest-excitement: "distress is suffered daily by all human beings, as they become tired, as they encounter difficulties in solving problems, as they interact with other human beings in ways which are less than ideal. **Distress is as general a negative affect as excitement is a positive one.** Between them they account for a major part of the posture of human beings towards themselves, towards each other, towards the world they live in" (2:48).

Fear-terror. Fear is a negative affect of greater toxicity than distress. Fear is activated by rapidly increasing neural firing that lies somewhere between the extremely quick response of surprise-startle and the more leisurely acceleration of interest-excitement. At very high levels of intensity (terror), this affect is acutely toxic. The feeling of fear arises from awareness of innate responses like bodily trembling, eyes that are open wide, a mouth that is agape, eyebrows that are raised, hair that stands on end, and a pallor that has drained the face of blood. The constancy of these responses (documented particularly well by Charles Darwin and widely agreed in the contemporary neurological literatures to be found in one form or another in most mammals) does not mean that fear is a unitary feeling. On the contrary, the phenomenology of fear is highly variegated: "one individual may characteristically feel fear in his face and stomach, another in an apparent tightening of his throat, another in an apparent band around his head, another in dizziness in his head, another in a weakness in his knees, another in a feeling of fear in his genitals, another in a feeling of fear in his anus, another in an accelerated heart rate, another in trembling of his face and limbs, another in a stiffening of all his muscles, another in sweating" (3:502). Similarly, fear varies considerably in relation to intensity, duration, and frequency: "One individual is vulnerable to constant low-grade fear. Another is frequently bombarded with slightly more intense fear but enjoys much positive affect in his fear-free intervals. Another is intensely afraid but with only moderate frequency. Yet another is entirely engulfed by terror" (3:521). Fear is subject to a wide variety of ideo-affective socializations, and theories (chapter 8) and scripts (chapter 9) emerge for individuals who attempt to control how much fear becomes magnified (i.e., how much it increases in duration and frequency). For example, a parent may think that a child, when afraid, should "tough it out." In such cases, the child may indeed learn to minimize fear, but only through the activation of shame or self-contempt at being a coward. Fear has been controlled, but perhaps at considerable cost.

Anger-rage. Anger is incited by incessant levels of stimulation, but at a higher intensity than in the case of distress. The faciality of anger is flushed and hot (in contrast to the pallor of fear), breathing is deep and rapid, vocalization is loud and sustained, the mouth is open, the jaw is clenched, and the eyes are narrowed: "it is the most urgent of all affects" (2:115). Importantly, there is no necessary relation between anger and aggression: "The infant may thrash about with flailing arms and limbs, as he may also do so, with less intensity, in distress. But there is no evidence of any innate coordinated action intended to aggress upon the source of the anger" (2:115). Nonetheless, anger, like fear, will become the target of extensive socialization, especially as its toxicity envelops not just the self but also the social world. Part of the difficulty we have in the management of anger is that it is both abstract (we may not know why we are angry or what has activated this particular scene of irritation) and general (it has a high degree of freedom in terms of its objects, duration, and intensity): "One can be angry for a moment, an hour, or a lifetime. One can be an angry child but a happy adult or a happy child but an angry adult. . . . I may wake mildly irritable in the morning and remain so for the rest of the day. Or one day I may not be at all angry until suddenly something makes me explode in rage" (3:116–17). While all affects can coassemble with each other, the abstractness and generality of anger are such that it is able to coassemble even with positive affects. In a 2011 interview with two of the creators of the then new Broadway musical *The Book of Mormon* (Trey Parker and Matt Stone, best known at that time for their work on the affectively promiscuous *South Park*), Jon Stewart says of the production that it is "so good it makes me fucking angry." Stewart's endorsement, which subsequently featured prominently in publicity for the show in the United States and the United Kingdom, is compelling not just because of the amplificatory pleasures of profanity but also because it is able to perform (as does the show itself) a persuasive composite of negative and positive feeling.

Shame-humiliation. The shame response is deeply mortifying: my eyes are averted, my head is turned down, I am blushing. I have reduced facial communication, and I am acutely self-conscious: "shame is the affect of indignity, of defeat, of transgression and of alienation" (2:118). While we might differentiate, colloquially, between shyness, shame, and guilt (and there has also been intense academic debate about the difference between shame and guilt, in particular), for Tomkins, these are all variations on the primary affect of shame-humiliation. Tomkins calls shame an affect auxiliary. What he means by this is that shame requires the prior activation of another, positive affect. Specifically, shame is triggered by the incomplete reduction of a positive affect like interest or enjoyment, leaving the self suspended between longing and despair: "I want, but—" (2:185). Because there are so many different ways in which interest or enjoyment might be inhibited, there are innumerable learned and unlearned sources of shame: "The experience of shame is inevitable for any human being insofar as desire outruns fulfillment sufficiently to attenuate interest without destroying it" (2:185). Indeed, the shame response seems to be an inevitable effect of intersubjective relations: "As soon as the infant learns to differentiate the face of the mother from the face of a stranger . . . , he is vulnerable to the shame response. . . . Under any schedule of socialization which is conceivable, the infant will sooner or later respond with shame rather than with excitement or enjoyment" (2:141–42). Paradoxically, while shame is a negative affect (it feels bad), it is a key affect in the maintenance of sociality: "shared shame [is] a prime instrument for strengthening the sense of mutuality and community whether it be between parent and child, friend and friend, or citizen and citizen. When one is ashamed of the other, that other is not only forced into shame but he is also reminded that the other is sufficiently concerned positively as well as negatively to feel ashamed of and for the other" (2:216). Tomkins's claim here is not that shame might be utilized, knowingly and affirmatively, in projects of social transformation or critique (as, for example, in the petitions for queer shame as an antidote to the conventionality of queer pride) but rather that sociality—the bonds that hold us together—is always brokered through shared and inevitable bad feeling.

Contempt. If shame is the affect of sociality, contempt is the affect of hierarchization: "contempt strengthens the boundaries and barriers between individuals and groups and is the instrument par excellence for the preservation of hierarchical, caste and class relationships" (2:216). Where shame is the experience of being suspended between what I want and what I can have, contempt is the definitive, sneering act of a self that has cut its ties to excitement and enjoyment. In shame, there is always a way back to the object or to positive affect; in contempt, the reduction of positive affect is complete: "I don't want" (2:232). Contempt is the least self-conscious of the negative affects, as it is primarily concerned, not with the mortifications of the self, but with the loathsome object (even when that object is the self, as in self-contempt). In the first two volumes of *AIC,* contempt was conjoined with disgust as different intensities of one affect: contempt-disgust. In volume 3, Tomkins explains the difficulties he encountered with such a formulation (e.g., contempt and disgust appear not to be weaker and stronger versions of the one affect in the way that fear-terror and anger-rage are), and he revises his idea that contempt is primary. He replaces contempt-disgust with the drive auxiliary responses disgust and dissmell. In this new formulation, contempt is a mixture of dissmell and anger.

Disgust and dissmell. Once Tomkins differentiates disgust and dissmell from contempt, he is able to reclassify them as responses that are auxiliary to the hunger, thirst, and oxygen drives: "Their function is clear. If the food about to be ingested activates dissmell, the upper lip and nose is [*sic*] raised and the head is drawn away from the apparent source of the offending odor. If the food has been taken into the mouth, it may, if disgusting, be spit out. If it has been swallowed and is toxic, it will produce nausea and be vomited out through either the mouth or nostrils. The early warning response via the nose is dissmell; the mouth or stomach response is disgust" (3:22). What makes disgust and dissmell affects rather than simply mechanisms auxiliary to the drives is that they signal strongly motivating feelings of rejection to both others and the self (self-disgust and self-dissmell). Moreover, both disgust and dissmell can be activated in response to nondigestive events: one can experience disgust or dissmell in response to dirty thoughts, for example.

One of the great advantages of Tomkins's model of the negative affects is that he is able to differentiate bad feeling in ways that have been lost in both the Freudian model of anxiety and aggression and the Deleuzian model of affects as prepersonal intensity. Both the Freudian and the Deleuzian models have plenty to contribute to thinking affectivity (and bad affect in particular), but what Tomkins's theory generates, perhaps uniquely in the contemporary scene, is a thick description of the life of affects as very specifically physiological, facial, individual, social, ideological, and parental. What is compelling for us is not that his descriptions of primary positive and negative affects can be verified empirically—they may or they may not; as we noted in the chapter on positive affects (chapter 5), we remain agnostic on this point. We take the categorical differences between good and bad affects to be the beginning, not the end, of an engaging analysis of affective life. Instead, what we find captivating in Tomkins's account of the primary affects is the way in which it is highly specific (shame is the incomplete reduction of interest or enjoyment, for example) yet also able to enumerate how the affects move, bind, borrow, compete, and combine with alacrity (shame, self-shame, disgust, self-disgust, dissmell, self-dissmell, contempt, and self-contempt).

FURTHER READING

The negative affects are most thoroughly examined in volume 2 (distress-anguish; shame-humiliation; contempt-disgust) and volume 3 (anger-rage; fear-terror) of *AIC*. There is a gap of twenty-seven years between these two volumes. In the preface to volume 3, Tomkins explains that the intensive focus on anger in that volume is due to the development of script theory (see chapter 9) in the intervening years. Much of this volume is concerned with how anger-laden scenes become magnified into scripts, for example, anger-management scripts, anger-control scripts, anger in depressive scripts, anger in disgust-decontamination scripts, antitoxic anger-avoidance scripts. In addition, Tomkins notes that since the publication of volume 2 in 1963, "the problems of ideology and violence have grown increasingly strident and urgent at the international level, prompting me to increase the depth and scope of my inquiry. The consequence is that most of Volume 3 concerns anger and violence" (3:xiv).

We also recommend Sedgwick and Frank's essay "Shame in the Cybernetic Fold," which has been very influential on how shame has been understood in queer studies and in the critical humanities and social sciences more broadly. Further work by Sedgwick on shame can be found in *Touching Feeling*.

INTERLUDE
TOMKINS AND SPINOZA

The name "Spinoza" does not show up even once in Silvan Tomkins's published writings, as far as we can tell. There is, nonetheless, a rich set of resonances between the seventeenth-century Dutch (Portuguese, Jewish) philosopher's thinking about the affects in his *Ethics* and Tomkins's thinking in *AIC*. Readers of these works side by side may be surprised to notice comparable intellectual dispositions as well as specific shared conceptualizations of affect. Among the former we would note a thoroughgoing naturalism that absents teleology from any account of the workings of nature, along with a vigorous commitment to complexity and compositionality in its accounts. Among the latter we have observed that both theorists conceive of affects as motives, relativize value to affect, and consider affect and knowledge of affect to be fundamental to human freedom. In this interlude, we offer a brief survey of these resonances. We will not, however, argue for a direct influence of Spinoza on Tomkins—although this is, to our minds, a distinct possibility. Rather, we offer the beginnings of an inquiry into the uptake and presence of Spinoza's (and Spinozist) ideas in the American philosophy and psychology in which Tomkins was schooled and on the American scene more generally.

Recent scholarship has attested to the presence of Spinoza's writing and thinking (despite its apparent absence) across a broad historical range in philosophical, political, and poetic texts of European Enlightenment thinkers, the English Romantics, and postwar French philosophy. Less is known about the reception of Spinoza in the United States. Clearly his theorization of affect in the *Ethics* was present to, if not exactly integrated into, the peculiar blend of philosophy and experimental psychology that would become characteristic of the American academy by the end of the nineteenth century. The philosopher George Stuart Fullerton's translation of the *Ethics* appeared in 1892, the same year that he hosted the first meeting of the American Psychological Association at the University of Pennsylvania. A quick glance at the indices of William James's essays and correspondence shows that James taught Spinoza at Harvard starting in 1890; in 1903 he would suggest the following exam question for a course on History of Philosophy: "Contrast Spinoza's Absolute with Hegel's" (*Correspondence of William James,* vol. 10, 246). George Santayana, a student of James who would become the most explicit proponent of Spinoza's ideas among the American philosophers, wrote an introduction to the Everyman's Library edition of the *Ethics* (1910). Edgar Singer Jr., a student of Fullerton and James, would later become one of Tomkins's professors. It is almost certain, then, that Tomkins, either as an undergraduate at the University of Pennsylvania (1927–30), or as a graduate student in psychology and philosophy at the same institution (1930–34), or, finally, as a postdoctoral fellow at Harvard would have read the *Ethics.*

In fact, it is likely that Tomkins, who grew up in New Jersey the son of Russian Jewish immigrants, would have sought out the work of the great Jewish heretic. Lewis Feuer suggests that "the group to whom Spinoza appealed most were the young Jewish intellectuals, children of the first generation of immigrants to America" who sought to identify with modernist scientific thinking and for whom Spinoza served as a "dramatic model" (336). Clearly Spinoza's own rejection of orthodox religious belief and commitment to naturalist explanation resonated powerfully with many young twentieth-century North American Jews who were shifting away from Old World piety and toward progressive ideals of all kinds. In thinking about this demographic shift, both generally and in the case of Tomkins, we should not underestimate the powerful contexts of American transcendentalism and pragmatism. Feuer notes, for example, that the Pulitzer Prize–winning historian Will Durant "began his career in 1913 as a popular lecturer at the Labor Temple on Second Avenue and Fourteenth Street" (338) with a lecture on Spinoza. This would eventually become a chapter of his immensely successful progressivist account of intellectual history, *The Story of Philosophy* (1926), which ends with a discussion of "Contemporary American Philosophers": Santayana, James, and John Dewey. Such lecture-circuit dissemination of pluralist ideals comes, in part, from earlier generations of American Romantic thinkers and writers who, it turns out, themselves borrowed from and transformed German and English uptakes of Spinoza. Consider one of Emerson's many references to Spinoza in his works: "Spinosa pronounced that there was but one substance;— yea, verily; but that boy yonder told me yesterday he thought the pinelog was God, and that God was in the jakes. What can Spinosa tell the boy?" (*Collected Works,* 9:104).

We offer this brief, potted historical survey to suggest that any thorough articulation of the relations between Tomkins's understanding of affect and Spinoza's would involve unearthing a transatlantic, American Spinoza. We can only gesture toward the existence and relevance of such a figure here. It seems to us that Emerson would have been much affected by the particular way that, in Spinoza's understanding, the "Mind" is an expression of the divine. Consider the introduction to part II of the *Ethics,* "Of the Nature and Origin of the Mind": "I pass now to explaining those things which must necessarily follow from the essence of God, or the infinite and eternal being—not, indeed, all of them . . . but only those that can lead us, by the hand, as it were, to the knowledge of the human mind and its highest blessedness" (115). The word "blessedness" appears here not simply as a reflexive gesture of piety but as a sly reference to Spinoza himself, whose name means "blessed"— Baruch, Benedito, Benedict. Spinoza explicitly asserts that the kind of knowledge he pursues ("of the human mind and its highest blessedness") is self-knowledge—that knowledge of (his) mind is knowledge of God, a kind of knowledge that is close to hand. What makes Spinoza fundamentally legible to the American Romantics is this epistemological and ontological mapping of mind onto nature such that knowledge of either one is, at the same time, knowledge of the other.

This Spinozist assertion becomes more problematic for post-Romantic science. It is notoriously difficult to follow and unfold Spinoza's careful, complex monism/pantheism and (what is often called) the "parallelism" of mind and body that accompanies it. Clearly, these ideas are not suited to conventionally empiricist sciences that disavow metaphysical concerns by assuming a reductive or eliminative materialism, or that disavow epistemological concerns by normatively defining the scientist's mind as a purely rational agent. Rather, Spinoza appears to offer support to those post-Romantic sciences, such as William James's radical empiricism or Freud's psychoanalysis, that are informed both by phenomenology and physiological psychology. These sciences invite a careful attention to the workings of the scientist's mind as itself a source of material, information, or data about the workings of the body, and vice versa. Recall, for Spinoza, "The object of the idea constituting the human mind is the body" (123), while knowledge of "the union of mind and body" depends on an adequate knowledge of "the nature of our body" (124). Spinoza's *Ethics* offers a framework for a nondualist philosophy that is committed to speculative knowledge of mind. But far from excluding empirical knowledge of bodies, such a speculative or theoretical account interimplicates knowledge of bodies with knowledge of mind.

A quest for a North American, post-Romantic, nonreductive, nondualist, speculative or theoretical psychological science that takes the physiology of bodies seriously: this is the broad context in which we can begin to track the resonances of Spinozist ideas in Tomkins's work. In this context, we observe, with some surprise, that Spinoza's speculations are compatible with several ideas that come primarily from biological systems theory (or second-order cybernetics) of the 1960s and 1970s: the notions of self-organization, emergence, and autopoeisis. Tomkins's own commitment to organized complexity took shape in his encounter with first-order cybernetics in the 1940s and 1950s (see chapter 12). For Tomkins, this commitment involves conceptualizing relations among and between nested systems that are in some ways dependent on, and in other ways independent of, one another. Spinoza, too, is committed to understanding the dynamics of complex systems—how, for example, these dynamics make questions of autonomy and freedom matters of degree. Consider this assertion: "in proportion as a body is more capable than others of doing many things at once, or being acted on in many ways at once, so its mind is more capable than others of perceiving many things at once" (124). Here Spinoza sketches out the ratio between bodily complexity (the capacity of a body to do many things at once or to be acted on in many ways at once) and perceptual complexity. He goes on to assert something similar of the relation between bodily autonomy and understanding: "And in proportion as the actions of a body depend more on itself alone, and as other bodies concur with it less in acting, so its mind is more capable of understanding distinctly" (124). Following this passage, Spinoza contends that "bodies are distinguished from one another by reason of motion and rest, speed and slowness, and not by reason of substance" (125). There is, no doubt, a genealogy of nonreductive materialism that Spinoza participates in here, one that would include ancient figures such as Democritus, Epicurus, and Lucretius. Perhaps this begins to account for the continuities in intellectual disposition with later cybernetics and biological systems theories. Rather than pursue these continuities in any detail, here we will simply point out that both Tomkins and Spinoza address the fundamentally dynamic, composite nature of bodies without reductionism, and both insist on the explanatory value of complexity.

In addition to these general intellectual dispositions, we have noticed some specific ideas that these thinkers share. Significantly, in their writing, affects are defined as both feelings and motives. We have seen how, for Tomkins, the affect system functions as the primary motivational system in humans and other animals and has evolved in conjunction with the biological drives. Spinoza offers a different but not incompatible definition: "By affect I understand affections of the body by which the body's power of acting is increased or diminished, aided or restrained, and at the same time, the ideas of these affections" (154). Note, first, how affects are at once of the body and of the mind, physiological changes ("affections of the body") that are also psychical events ("ideas of these affections"). This dovetails neatly with Tomkins's insistence on the nature of affects as both irreducibly physiological (neurological as well as gross anatomical changes, for instance, a cold sweat) and irreducibly psychical (say, the experience of fear). Either way, affect is part of larger causal sequences. Spinoza puts it this way: "So experience itself, no less clearly than reason, teaches that men believe themselves free because they are conscious of their own actions, and ignorant of the causes by which they are determined, that the decisions of the mind are nothing but the appetites themselves, which therefore vary as the disposition of the body varies. For each one governs everything from his affect" (157). Tomkins's understanding of causation, coming after developments in statistical mechanics and the notion of circular causality, is different from Spinoza's more linear model of determination. Nevertheless, both thinkers consider the affects to be those governing agents that fundamentally motivate human behavior, that increase and diminish the body's power to act.

As a crucial consequence of this prioritizing of affect, both thinkers relativize value. Here is Spinoza: "it is clear that we neither strive for, nor will, neither want, nor desire anything because we judge it to be good; on the contrary, we judge something to be good because we strive for it, will it, want it, and desire it" (160). And here is Tomkins's almost identically radical assertion: "**It is our theory of value that for human subjects value is any object of human affect.** Whatever one is excited by, enjoys, fears, hates, is ashamed of, is contemptuous of or is distressed by is an object of value, positive or negative" (1:329). This epistemological and ontological prioritizing of affect is a key aspect of both thinkers' thoroughgoing naturalism and should contribute significantly to any attempt to offer a nontranscendental account of value. For Spinoza as well for Tomkins, value is a function of history, accident, and power. (We can glimpse how important Spinoza's relativizing of value was for Nietzsche's turn toward a genealogy of value.) Spinoza's oft-noted relativism was one reason his thinking was rejected so virulently. What has not been noticed is how the opening up of value to history depends on a specific relation between affects and objects. We have already discussed what Tomkins calls the freedom of object of the affect system, that is, the fact that any affect may have any object. Spinoza puts the same idea this way: "Anything can be the accidental cause of joy, sadness, or desire" (162). Indeed, the fundamental complexity of the affects in our thinking and feeling lives is, in part, a consequence of this basic freedom of object. Both thinkers conceive of such complexity along similar lines: compare Tomkins's discussion of "affect-object reciprocity" (1:133–34) with Spinoza's discussion of the objects of our love or hate (163–64). And, for both thinkers, the complexity of the relations between affects, their objects, and their causes can be analyzed or thought. Such analysis of affect can bring knowledge of how we come to judge things to be good or bad.

Finally, and relatedly, what motivates both Spinoza's and Tomkins's careful, insistent, and exhaustive thinking about the affects is the fundamental therapeutic value of self-knowledge. For both, knowledge of affect is a condition for understanding how we are free and unfree. In parts IV and V of the *Ethics,* Spinoza addresses human bondage and human freedom, and although it would seem that he aligns "the power of the affects" with bondage and "the power of the intellect" with freedom, the nitty-gritty details of his writing do not bear out this too-simplified alignment. Indeed, for Spinoza, the limitations of reason motivate his project: "it is necessary to come to know both our nature's power and its lack of power, so that we can determine what reason can do in moderating the affects, and what it cannot do" (208). Reason cannot, for example, restrain affect; an affect can only be restrained by a stronger affect. Despite its limitations as governing agent, however, there are some things that reason can do, and do well: sift and separate, identify, clarify. Reason can separate emotions "from the thought of an external cause" (247) and, by dislinking affects from objects, disable passions that diminish our power. Spinoza puts it this way: "the more an affect is known to us, then, the more it is in our power, and the less the mind is acted on by it" (247). Knowledge of the affects, the project of the *Ethics,* increases human freedom by permitting us to convert passions (that diminish our power) into actions (that increase it). This is the "remedy" (248) Spinoza offers, a remedy broadly reminiscent of any therapeutic project (such as psychoanalysis) that aims, not to rid ourselves of problematic affective dynamics, but to know them and, in knowing them, create the possibility of unfixing their hold on us. What Tomkins shares with Spinoza is the commitment to understanding how humans are governed by (our) affects, for better and for worse, and how we can think about, and live with, such forms of governance.

FURTHER READING

We used Edwin Curley's translation of the *Ethics* in preparing this chapter. For scholarship on the place of Spinoza in eighteenth- and nineteenth-century European literature and philosophy, see especially Jonathan Israel's *Radical Enlightenment: Philosophy and the Making of Modernity* (2001), Marjorie Levinson's "A Motion and a Spirit: Romancing Spinoza" (2007) (see her remarks on the similarities of Spinoza's work to aspects of biological systems theory), and the essays collected in *The New Spinoza* (1997). On the reception of Spinoza in the United States, see Benjamin Wolstein's "The Romantic Spinoza in America" (1953) and Lewis S. Feuer's "Spinoza's Thought and Modern Perplexities: Its American Career" (1995). We tracked multiple mentions of Spinoza in Ralph Waldo Emerson's *Collected Works,* in *The Correspondence of William James,* and in several collections of James's essays, including *Some Problems of Philosophy, Essays in Philosophy,* and *Essays in Radical Empiricism.* Wayne Boucher's *Spinoza in English: A Bibliography from the Seventeenth Century to the Present* helped us to locate several other historical and popular treatments of Spinoza's philosophy: George Santayana's "Ethical Doctrines of Spinoza" (1886), George Stuart Fullerton's *The Philosophy of Spinoza* (1892), Will Durant's *The Story of Philosophy* (1927), and others.

Antonio Damasio may be thought of as an inheritor of a speculative approach that interimplicates knowledge of bodies with knowledge of mind (see *Looking for Spinoza: Joy, Sorrow, and the Feeling Brain*). The best philosophical explications of Spinoza we have seen are Gilles Deleuze's in his works *Expressionism in Philosophy* and *Spinoza: Practical Philosophy*.

PART II

IMAGERY

7
IMAGES

While *affect* is clearly the most important term in Silvan Tomkins's *AIC,* *imagery* is a not-too-distant second, serving to connect a cluster of concepts that we address here in part II. For Tomkins, imagery is the material of memory and perception, a kind of phenomenological mindstuff that, when amplified by affect and transformed by cognition, becomes organized into theories, scripts, and ideologies. Here we introduce Tomkins's understanding of imagery by unfolding some aspects of his cybernetic model of neural communication. We then discuss Images, a notion related to but (somewhat confusingly, given their similar nomenclature) distinct from imagery. Images, for Tomkins, act as blueprints for the human feedback system: they give purpose to thought, feeling, and action. Finally, we explore a subclass of Images, what Tomkins calls the General Images, blueprints specific to the human affect system that generate some of our most powerful, contradictory experiences.

Tomkins introduces the notion of imagery in the first few pages of *AIC1* in a discussion of "information duplicating mechanisms in human beings" (1:10). His cybernetic account begins from this premise: "We conceive of man . . . as an inter- and intra-communication system, utilizing feedback networks which transmit, match and transform, information in analogical form and in the form of messages in a language. By a communication system we mean a mechanism capable of regular and systematic duplication of something in space and time" (1:9). In humans and other organisms, sensory receptors duplicate "certain aspects of the world surrounding the receptors" (1:10), and this information, primarily analog in form, is then duplicated again and again via afferent nerves and transmitted further into the organism. In mobile and more complex organisms, there is a receiving station at which there occurs an additional kind of duplication, "an as yet unknown process we will call *transmuting*" (1:10), that turns the analog information into a conscious report. Consciousness, for Tomkins, "is a unique type of duplication by which some aspects of the world reveal themselves to another part of the same world. . . . The uniqueness of this transformation has been a source of discomfiture for the psychologist" (1:10). Note how, in this pleasingly understated version of the problem of consciousness, Tomkins avoids a transcendentalizing break or cut between consciousness and the world. He seeks, rather, to create a model that maintains continuity between consciousness and its objects.

At the same time, Tomkins does not reject what he calls the "Kantian strategy." To account for perceptual learning—the fact that the organism learns to perceive and compose its world through trial and error—he introduces something that resembles Kantian discontinuity: "It is our belief that the afferent sensory information is not directly transformed into a conscious report. What is consciously perceived is *imagery* which is created by the organism itself. . . . **The world we perceive is a dream we learn to have from a script we have not written**" (1:13). This last sentence, which appears several times in Tomkins's writings, offers a highly compressed summary of his understanding of imagery. A key component of this understanding is a mechanism that matches afferent (incoming) sensory, motor, or other information with efferent (outgoing) central feedback:

> Before any sensory message becomes conscious it must be *matched by a centrally innervated feedback mechanism*. This is a central efferent process which attempts to duplicate the set of afferent messages at the central receiving station . . . matching the constantly changing sensory input is a skill that one learns as one learns any skill. It is this skill which eventually supports the dream and the hallucination, in which central sending produces the conscious image in the absence of afferent support. (1:13)

This challenging, underexplored aspect of Tomkins's theory remains speculative in his writing (just as his neural model of affect remains speculative). But we consider it to be promising insofar as it offers a conceptual means to navigate between the Scylla of constructionism and the Charybdis of realism. Tomkins insists that what we perceive is a skilled construction based on sensory (and other) input: imagery is both centrally emitted and connected to the periphery (and other parts) of the organism via the information duplicating mechanisms that run between our sensory receptors and our central nervous system. "It [i.e., the world we perceive] is neither our capricious construction nor a gift we inherit without work" (1:13), or as he puts it later in a different context, "it is the external world that is the teacher of the language of the internal world" (4:334) (see chapter 12 for more on these aspects of Tomkins's approach to consciousness).

While the idea of "centrally emitted imagery" appears several times in *AIC1*, Tomkins's most extended discussion takes place in a chapter in *AIC4* ("The Lower Senses") on the body image and phantom limbs. Examples of phantom limb phenomena show up with some frequency in the history of modern philosophy, from Descartes's *Meditations* to German phenomenological writings of the 1890s, often alongside discussions of hallucination and dreaming as somewhat marginal examples that pose problems for theories of sensation and perception. By contrast, Tomkins places phantom limbs at the center of his perceptual theory. After reviewing the twentieth-century psychological literature on the subject, he proposes that "the reality and stability of the phantom limb we regard as evidence that what is normally perceived is a centrally innervated image, guided by sensory input but also by memory" (4:250). Tomkins argues that "perceiving is not partly some mediate process but entirely so and . . . uses the feedback-matching principle" (4:251), and he powerfully suggests that **all conscious experience is some type of imagery but not necessarily the same type of imagery** (4:252). Often enough, we can distinguish imagery whose ultimate source lies outside our bodies, such as sensory (visual, auditory, olfactory) imagery, from imagery whose source is internal (memories, beliefs, desires). Sometimes (more or less often) "the individual can mistake primarily inner-guided imagery for the outer-guided imagery" (4:253), resulting in uncertainty or, in more extreme cases, hallucination. Consider the example of a smell that you have difficulty placing, that may in fact be a memory image rather than primarily a sensory one. Or consider the interesting example of judging whether a recent acquaintance is "your type," which involves a complex movement between inner- and outer-guided imagery.

Phantom limb phenomena, according to Tomkins, emerge from a conflict between different kinds of imagery: inner-guided kinesthetic (and other) memory imagery of the limb overrides outer-guided visual imagery that offers evidence of its absence. Other explanations account for the phantom by way of an entirely afferent process, such as the irritation of severed nerve endings. But Tomkins suggests that phantoms exist primarily because "there has been voluminous, continuous stimulation from the inner receptors both preceding and following purposive action with the limbs" (4:257). That is, phantoms are a consequence of learning how to move and use our bodies (learning to stand, walk, run, catch, and so on), skills that result from central feedback matching. The important point, for Tomkins, is that phantom limbs make figural what is more usually experienced as ground: the body image that always accompanies us, a result of vestibular and kinesthetic stimulation, report, and matching. The figural experience of the body image in phantom limbs lets Tomkins move toward a general theory of perception as it comprises varieties of imagery.

If it is not always easy to follow Tomkins's discussions of imagery, it may in part be due to his commitment to a technical cybernetic account. In a chapter on "The Feedback Mechanism: Consciousness, the Image, and the Motoric," Tomkins offers a detailed examination of a neural communication process in the hypothetical case of someone throwing a dart at a target (one of his recurring examples). He sketches the complex feedback relations among and between sensory receptor cells, transmuted reports, centrally emitted transmissions that stimulate motor nerves, and the monitoring processes that identify outcomes and consequences (4:324–32). "The individual who learns how to achieve outer targets is also learning how to use his neurological networks" (4:330), asserts Tomkins, whose fundamental point appears to be the following: "Paradoxically, it is only by 'outer' exploration that the inner space is ultimately mapped" (4:330). Here Tomkins insists on one of the basic tenets of biological systems theory—that the distinction between organism and environment reappears and is made use of within the organism itself: "the external world must be reproduced within this [neural] circuitry if it is to be assimilable and useful to the individual so that ultimately the dichotomy between the inner and outer domain becomes a dichotomy within the inner world" (4:334). Again, we see Tomkins's navigation of both the continuity and discontinuity between organism and environment: "we do not embrace solipsism . . . any more than does the biochemist who studies the transformations that are necessary before foodstuffs can be used by the body" (4:334). Internalizing the system–environment distinction is a condition for learning and makes it possible for an organism to meet its needs and attain its ends.

That humans (and other animals) have purposes, and that they do, sometimes, achieve these purposes: Tomkins accommodates this significant fact by introducing the idea of "a centrally emitted blueprint which we call the *Image*" (1:17). The Image may be built from sensory, memory, and other kinds of imagery, but it is nevertheless distinct from them:

> In sensory and memory matching the model is given by the world as it exists now in the form of sensory information, and as it existed once before in the form of memory information. In the case of the Image the individual is projecting a possibility which he hopes to realize or duplicate and that must precede and govern his behavior if he is to achieve it. This Image of an end state to be achieved may be compounded of memory or perceptual images or any combination or transformation of these. It may be a state which is both conscious and unconscious, vague or clear, abstract or concrete, transitory or enduring, one or many, conjoint or alternative in structure. (1:17)

In Tomkins's example, a dart thrower who aims to hit a target develops an Image that combines visual and kinesthetic imagery to guide her throw—a clear, concrete, transitory Image. Here's a more complicated example: a pianist working on a piece of music (from a classical repertoire, say) develops an Image that combines auditory imagery (from recordings and performances she has heard), kinesthetic imagery (her piano technique), affective imagery (a specific arc of feeling, say), and her cognitive understanding of the piece. The abstract Image she develops may begin somewhat vaguely but becomes clearer as she refines her idea. Perhaps it eludes consciousness or is difficult to put into words. Eventually satisfied with her interpretation, she may try to achieve this Image in public performance. An attentive listener may hear the music in a new, perhaps enduring way. "An Image comes to control and monitor the feedback process" (1:20), proposes Tomkins, which permits us to try to achieve our aims, whatever these may be. Of course, there is never any guarantee of success.

At this point, a reader may be wondering how, in Tomkins's understanding, Images developed to guide and give purpose to the organism interact with affects, which do not obey the means–end difference. As we hope to have made clear in part I, Tomkins is entirely committed to a noninstrumental account of affect. In *AIC3*, he insists on distinguishing his theory of motivation from any account that assumes that "motivation is best understood as involving means and ends and that ends are what means are 'for'" (3:66). Affect, he asserts, is not "a carrot useful primarily in persuading us to perform instrumental acts. . . . Affect is an end in itself, with or without instrumental behavior" (3:66–67). Nonetheless, *affects crucially motivate the construction of Images that give purpose to the human feedback system.* We find Tomkins's distinction between affect as motive and Image as purpose to be very helpful: **"The Image is a blueprint for the feedback mechanism: as such it is purposive and directive. Affect we conceive of as a motive, by which we mean immediately rewarding or punishing experience"** (1:122). This distinction emerges from his cybernetic account of information flows within the organism. Consider, while much sensory or motor information in the organism is "motivationally neutral" (1:20), signals from the drive and affect systems are not neutral: "they are immediately 'acceptable' or 'unacceptable' without prior learning" (1:20) and, in this way, "gradually become targets for the feedback control system" (1:21). (Tomkins emphasizes how gradual this process is.) Affects and drives color and amplify some imagery that is then compounded by the central feedback mechanism into Images or purposes. Structurally independent of one another, Images and affects are crucially related in the gradual development of an organism's goals.

Consider a reflexive example that may help to convey both the distinction between and relation among affects and Images. One feeling that motivated the authors to plan and write the book you are currently reading was a dissatisfaction with the ways that Tomkins's work was either misunderstood or underused by colleagues and students in the humanities and social sciences. We were perplexed by how few scholars took up Tomkins's thinking in any detail as well as somewhat frustrated by how the term *affect* was most often used in a post-Deleuzian sense, for we thought (and continue to think) that Tomkins offers a generative vocabulary and set of tools for theoretically sophisticated, politically minded criticism. These specific feelings (of dissatisfaction, perplexity, and frustration, complex emotions rooted in the affects of distress, surprise, and anger) motivated our commitment to write a book that unfolded Tomkins's ideas. Only then did we develop a specific Image or goal, that of a portable handbook that serves as a useable introduction to Tomkins's ideas. Note, the Image that has guided our writing is independent of the feelings that motivated it (we might have developed a different goal for a book on Tomkins, a biography, for example). But we would never have developed any Image without such feelings.

Tomkins offers an extended treatment of the relation between Images and affects in discussions of what he calls the General Images (1:327–35, 2:261–300). Four Images, he proposes, provide general guidance to the affect system as a whole: **"(1) Positive affect should be maximized; (2) Negative affect should be minimized; (3) Affect inhibition should be minimized; (4) Power to maximize positive affect, to minimize negative affect, and to minimize affect inhibition should be maximized"** (1:328). Although Tomkins does not consider these to be innate, he suggests that, given the structure of the affect system in human beings, there is a very high probability that the General Images will develop. Once they do, they come into conflict with one another. For a simple example, the goal of maximizing the enjoyment of rich foods clashes with the goal of minimizing the distress associated with indigestion. Conflicts such as these generate much of the complexity of human experience and become the hidden ground for ethical, religious, and political debates about how life should be lived. (In the preceding sentence, substitute "commodity culture" and "exploitation of labor" for "rich foods" and "indigestion.") Tomkins proposes that "such debates are ordinarily conducted as if they were entirely independent of the affective basis of human reward and punishment" (1:329), and it is in this context that he asserts, "It is our theory of value that for human subjects value is any object of human affect" (1:329). In our discussion of Spinoza and Tomkins, we pointed out how these two thinkers both relativize value to affect. As Tomkins puts it, "value hierarchies result from value conflicts wherein the same object is both loved and hated, both exciting and shaming, both distressing and enjoyable" (1:329). It is primarily the four General Images that create such rampant conflicts of affect, and therefore of value, within and among individuals, groups, cultures, and civilizations. (We will see in chapter 10 how ideology, as Tomkins develops that concept in *AIC3*, works to resolve these fundamental conflicts.) As usual, we will have to be highly selective in our summary of Tomkins's writing. We think there are both interesting parallels and differences between Tomkins's discussion of the third General Image ("minimize affect inhibition") and the psychoanalytic notion of repression. On one hand, it would seem that Tomkins supports Freud's idea that the inhibition of affect produces symptomatic distortion: "The inhibition of the overt expression of any affect will ordinarily produce a residual form of the affect which is at once heightened, distorted, and chronic and which is severely punitive" (1:330). (In this context, Tomkins points to the role of alcohol as "self-administered therapy of affect inhibition" [1:331].) However, in a longer discussion in *AIC2* of the conflicts between the third and first two General Images, Tomkins offers a more nuanced understanding in which "inhibited affects may sometimes be effectively suppressed without residual intensification" (2:267) or may coexist alongside a defensive, attenuating response. For example, "the cry of distress may be experienced in the distorted form of the stiff upper lip, which is calculated to interfere with the trembling crying mouth" (2:267). Here Tomkins translates psychoanalytic insights concerning repression of the drives into the terms of his theory: the affects themselves serve to inhibit and suppress, as well as to amplify and magnify, one another, creating self-division and conflict, an "alien force deep within every self" (2:269). Interestingly, for Tomkins, neither the expression of affect nor its inhibition can serve as a necessary index or guide to identifying repression: "There is no necessary relation between expression and intensity or duration of affects, or between suppression and intensity or duration of affects" (2:282). Rather, expression and suppression of affect will depend on which particular affect theories and scripts are developed, theories that may differ between individuals, groups, and cultures. We discuss Tomkins's notions of theory and script (in chapters 8 and 9) as they offer complementary alternatives to developmental models in psychoanalysis.

Tomkins's discussion of the fourth General Image, that of maximizing power, offers some useful, sweeping generalizations: "whenever human beings wish ends in themselves, they sooner or later recruit the auxiliary wishes to be able to command the means, whatever they may be, that are necessary to achieve those ends" (2:290). Indeed, for Tomkins, the idea of God derives from the power Image, as does "the idea of progress, with its derivatives—the conquest of nature and the rights of man" (2:292). Tomkins offers several political insights that, published in 1963, still seem to have resonance. For example, here is one description of a postcolonial affective condition: "in the present worldwide revolution, we may expect the emergence of counter-humiliation, counter-terror and counter-distress in repayment of the former colonial powers for past suffering, past terror and, above all, past humiliation" (2:299). Or consider what happens when the "power strategy" becomes "monopolistic":

> Nothing is more commonplace than the self-defeating investment in the means to any end. . . . The excitement of the quest for knowledge can be transformed into the drudgery of scholarship. . . . The enjoyment of intimacy between parents and children can be surrendered by the effort of the breadwinner to guarantee the economic future of that family. . . . In the investment of affect in the acquisition of money, the universal means to ends of many kinds, original affective investments in ends in themselves may become liquidated or attenuated so that the pursuit of the means becomes an end in itself. (2:292–93)

When the power Image outweighs the other General Images, Tomkins tells us, we see fantasies of escape, role reversal, and revenge as well as the conversion of affect into an end in itself. It is hard not to think of contemporary electoral campaigns in this context.

Given their relative importance in the first two volumes of *AIC,* it is curious to note that the General Images do not initially appear to have the same profile in Tomkins's later writing. But it is possible to find references to them in his writing on ideology as well as on "the polarity scale," his affective measure of the left–right spectrum in politics. In fact, Tomkins's understanding of imagery and Images is in the background of much of his writing of the 1970s and 1980s. As he puts it in *AIC4,* "it is only when the pervasive role of imagery is appreciated, not only in the interpretation of sensory information in the construction of the perceptual world, but also in the control of the feedback mechanism via the image, that the problem of imagery assumes a central significance for psychological theory. It is through private images that the individual builds the public world that enables both social consensus and competence in dealing with the physical world" (4:284). And, we would add, such "private images" also create social dissensus and incompetence in dealing with the political world. It is a virtue of Tomkins's theory of imagery that it permits an integrated approach to so many kinds and aspects of world construction.

FURTHER READING

Tomkins's writing on imagery and the General Images is distributed throughout various volumes of *AIC*. In the first two volumes, we refer interested readers to "Introduction: Consciousness and Affect in Behaviorism and Psychoanalysis" (chapter 1), "Affect Dynamics" (chapter 9), and "The Impact of Humiliation: General Images and Strategies" (chapter 19). In the last volumes, we consulted "Affect and Cognition: 'Reasons' as Coincidental Causes of Affect Evocation" (chapter 2), "Perception: Defining Characteristics—Central Matching of Imagery" (chapter 10), "The Lower Senses" (chapter 11), "The Higher Senses" (chapter 12), and "The Feedback Mechanism: Consciousness, the Image, and the Motoric" (chapter 14).

For more on Tomkins's approach to imagery and phantom limbs in specific relation to Freud's writing on the uncanny, see Adam Frank's "Phantoms Limn: Silvan Tomkins and Affective Prosthetics" (2007).

We note here that Ruth Leys's reductive characterization of Tomkins's theory as "anti-intentionalist" overlooks the fundamental role for imagery in his account of motivation. Imagery, as mental representation that can be either conscious or unconscious, is clearly intentional in the phenomenological sense.

8
THEORY, WEAK AND STRONG

What is an affect theory? What does it do?

In their introduction to *The Affect Theory Reader,* Gregory Seigworth and Melissa Gregg survey the many different ways that affect can be theorized: these theories might be phenomenological, cybernetic, Spinozist, psychoanalytic, cognitive, Darwinian, literary, neurological, or some combination thereof. By this reckoning, an affect theory is a conceptual schema that explains to its readers how affects work, how we might best study and apprehend them, and how we might anticipate their transmission in the future. We can claim, unproblematically, that Spinoza has a theory of affect and that Darwin has a differently oriented theory of the emotions, and (if we dig around a little) we might also find a theory of affect in the writings of Freud ("the vicissitude of the quota of affect . . . is far more important than the vicissitude of the idea" ["Repression," 153]). Similarly, we can find any number of scientific theories that gather data and test hypotheses about the affects. A neurologist, for example, might elaborate a theory about how emotion is regulated by various subcortical parts of the brain and the prefrontal cortex. Additionally, a political theory of affect might allow us to track how emotion operates in electoral systems; a psychologist might turn to theories of affect to map out new genealogies of embodiment; a literary critic might develop theories of minor and ugly feelings to think about class, race, and gender in late modernity.

For Tomkins, one important kind of affect theory is missing from this inventory: the personal ideo-affective organizations that are established through socialization and that give shape and dynamism to an individual's everyday life. Tomkins calls these perceptual–ideo-affective–motor organizations *affect theories,* and he sees these ways of organizing the experience of one's own affects in daily life as broadly homologous to the affect theories that a neurologist or geographer or literary critic might employ. The similarity between a scientific theory and an individual affect theory is particularly compelling for Tomkins—like scientists, individuals use available data to form hypotheses, forecast possible outcomes, and develop strategies for coping with affective events:

we have used the word theory to stress the high-order inferential processes which are inevitably involved when a human being is engaged by affect. The co-ordinations of percepts, ideas and actions which are prompted by even the most transitory affects are of the same general order as those involved in science in the co-ordination of empirical evidence and theory. **The individual whose affect is engaged is inevitably thereby confronted with such questions as: "What is happening?" "What is going to happen?" "How sure am I of what seems to be happening and what will happen?" "What should I do?"** These are theoretical questions in that they involve the interpretation of empirical evidence, the extrapolation into the future, the evaluation of both interpretation and extrapolation and the application of knowledge to strategy. (2:369)

There are two different ways, then, that we could talk about Darwin's affect theories. There is the account given in *The Expression of the Emotions in Man and Animals* in which Darwin offers an evolutionary explanation of the manifestation of emotion in humans—an account built on data delivered to him by a global network of correspondents. And then there are the affect theories that subtend his (Charles's) everyday life—theories given form (as they are for the rest of us) by the vicissitudes of socialization as well as familial, historical, and geographical milieux. It is because these two kinds of affect theories are not wholly independent of each other that Tomkins is often interested in the biographies of figures like Darwin or Freud or Chekhov or Marx or Wittgenstein or Hemingway (see chapter 13). Tacking back and forth between Darwin's scientific theory of affect and his personal affect theory, Tomkins notes,

The affect of interest or excitement is, paradoxically, absent from Darwin's catalogue of emotions. Although Darwin dealt with surprise and meditation the more sustained affect of interest per se was somehow overlooked. Darwin's own primary affective investments in perceiving and in thinking may well have attenuated his awareness of his own sustained excitement in exploration, so that he misidentified the affect with the function of thinking. (1:337–38)

Tomkins's interest in conjugating formal affect theories and individual affect theories is not psychobiographical in any conventional or reductive sense (see chapter 13); rather, his use of the term *theory* to describe the way people cope with the affective flux of their own experience and life draws directly from the rich personological work that he undertook at the Harvard Psychological Clinic with Henry Murray (see chapter 11).

An affect theory, in this Tomkinsian sense of an individual's ideoaffective organization, has two components: first, the "cognitive antenna" (2:319) that examines incoming information and assesses the relevance of that information for a particular affect, and second, a set of strategies for coping with (although not necessarily avoiding) affective experience, especially negative affective experience. That is, affect theories are responses to the world as we encounter and imagine it. They are the means by which we negotiate the affective traffic of everyday life and the defenses that we use to survive turbulence or sudden and distressing changes of circumstances. These affect theories emerge from patterns of rewarding or punitive socialization of a particular affect. Take shame as an example—as a child, I may have been made to feel ashamed of my shame; or my shame may have been frequently amplified into humiliation by those closest to me; or my shame may have been abruptly curtailed by another's anger ("Hold your head up!," "Don't be a cry-baby!"). In all these cases, the socialization of shame has been punishing and I have likely developed a *strong shame theory*: I will experience shame and humiliation in relation to a large number of situations and stimuli; I will come to anticipate shame and humiliation around every corner; I will become preoccupied with managing humiliation across most parts of my life. Or, perhaps I have been fortunate as a child: my shame has been recognized, attenuated and tolerated. In this latter case, Tomkins argues, I am likely to develop a *weak shame theory*:

> In general the rewarding socialization of shame and contempt has the consequence of producing a weak shame theory.... **It accounts for little more than itself.** It is developed to account for and

organize very specific experiences which are neither intense enough nor recurrent enough to prompt the generation of more than a crude general description of the phenomena themselves. (2:312)

A weak theory is sufficiently well targeted at potentially aversive events that the duration and intensity of those events is minimized. In the light of a weak shame theory I will tend not to dwell on feelings of indignity; I am less likely to magnify, cognitively elaborate, or embellish shame into mortification or humiliation. To call a shame theory weak, then, is not to say that it is ineffective. On the contrary, in order to stay weak these kinds of ideo-affective organizations must be effective in their management of negative affects. To call an affect theory weak is to say that it remains close to the events at hand, it generates an account of my experience that is good enough for current needs. In this way, a weak theory operates silently to guide action in a way that minimizes one's exposure to toxic, negative feeling.

One of Tomkins's favorite examples of the efficacy of a weak affect theory is a weak fear theory. Imagine that you are standing at the curb of a busy street, waiting to cross. As you pause to assess the traffic, you are unbothered by fear. Your weak fear theory enables you to act *as if* you were afraid (you hesitate) but without the conscious experience of noxious feeling:

> The affect theory (a fear theory) here operates so silently and effectively that it would surprise everyman if the question of fear about crossing the street were even to be raised. He would say, quite self-persuasively, that he uses his common sense so that he doesn't need to be afraid. This is one of the major functions of any negative affect theory—to guide action so that negative affect is not experienced. **It is affect acting at a distance.** Just as human beings can learn to avoid danger, to shun the flame before one is burnt, so also can they learn to avoid shame or fear before they are seared by the experience of such negative affect. (2:320)

A strong affect theory, on the other hand, emerges when a weak theory breaks down and is no longer effective. When a weak theory fails, it may become strong through what Tomkins calls psychological magnification (see chapter 9). A strong fear theory bodes ill for the everyday management of feeling, and it may indicate serious psychopathology in which fear has become a ubiquitous feature of an individual's encounters with others and with the world:

> a negative affect theory gains in strength, paradoxically, by virtue of the continuing failures of its strategies to afford protection through successful avoidance of the experience of negative affect . . . it is the repeated and apparently uncontrollable spread of the experience of negative affect which prompts the increasing strength of the ideo-affective organization which we have called a strong affect theory. Despite the fact that a strong affect theory may eventually succeed in preventing the experience of negative affect, it is usually only through the repeated failure to achieve this end that the ideo-affective organization grows stronger. (2:323–24)

Like a scientific theory, our affect theories undergo constant revision—new data are added, new experiences are calibrated against existing models, different affect theories (fear, shame, excitement) are tested against each other. Most often, Tomkins argues, affect theories coexist, or compete with each other, or find some kind of mutual accommodation. Sometimes, however, these affective strategies break down. Tomkins calls a particularly strong affect theory *monopolistic*. In these circumstances, one affect (e.g., shame) has come to dominate the life of an individual, ensnaring him or her in a monochromatic world of humiliation ("In a monopolistic humiliation theory all roads lead from perception, cognition and action to humiliation, and all roads lead back from humiliation to all the other sub-systems. It is an organization in which wherever one looks, whatever one thinks, whatever one does, humiliation may be aroused" [2:424]). While these monopolistic theories are strong, they are not uniform:

> We might say that humiliation theory is monopolistic when any one or any combination of sub-systems is entirely and continuously captured by this affect. We might say humiliation becomes monopolistic when the individual never experiences humiliation because he is forever vigilant and so always successfully avoids the feeling

of shame. We might consider humiliation monopolistic whenever the individual is perpetually humiliated, as we define an anxiety neurosis by the presence of chronic anxiety. We might define it by the exclusive interpretation of stimuli in terms of their relevance for humiliation, independent of whether this leads to humiliation or to successful avoidance of the affective experience. Any one of these, or any combination, might be an appropriate way to define monopolistic humiliation theory. (2:379)

Monopolistic affect theories are central to Tomkins's understanding of severe psychological dysfunctions like schizophrenia or paranoia. In these conditions, the individual has been captured by strong, monopolistic shame and fear theories that color every part of his or her life. The consequent humiliation and terror produce excessive levels of vigilance and usually futile attempts at defense: "the individual has no holidays from the unfinished and unfinishable business of coping with humiliation" (2:425). In these cases, there is an overorganization between the subsystems of personality (cognition, perception, action, thinking, memory are all coordinated in their efforts to ward off this particularly toxic feeling), and there is an overinterpretation of the available experiential data (everything now feels humiliating or terrorizing): all parts of the personality are now on permanent alert, and the human being is seriously constricted in terms of his or her affective and cognitive function.

Because the pervasiveness of an affect here and now is relatively independent of what can happen to that affect over time, Tomkins also thinks of affect theories developmentally (how they may change from childhood to adulthood). An affect theory that continues to get stronger over time is said to *snowball*; here early experiences become more potent, and they come to govern personality and its subsystems more and more. By describing the developmental or chronological trajectories of an affect theory, Tomkins is able to introduce a significant amount of variegation into his account: early monopolistic theories may attenuate rather than snowball, for example, or a weakly organized affect theory may intensify into monopolism late in life. Additionally, there may be times when an affect theory that is a relatively minor part of personality encroaches into the individual's everyday life, displacing other prevailing affects. Tomkins calls this an *intrusion* model of affect. For example, a usually sanguine individual may become contemptuous or angry when drunk, or a mostly fearless person may become terrified at the dentist. This vulnerability to specific affects in certain circumstances may be a constant part of an individual's personality, or it may be that in an otherwise emotionally steady life, extraordinary circumstances (a death, or loss, or illness) provoke the abrupt intrusion from the past of affective experiences that are distressing or overwhelming and that feel completely alien (as in an acute psychotic episode). Tomkins calls this later event an example of an *iceberg* model of affect, and he notes that because psychoanalytic theories tend to think primarily in terms of development, they have overemphasized snowball and iceberg models of affect, at the expense of the other kinds of affective models that structure our lives.

Tomkins presents this typology of basic affect theories as a specific critique of the Freudian emphasis on development. To return to the example of a weak fear theory (you are standing at the curb, waiting to cross the street), the ideo-affective organization that Tomkins would call a weak fear theory enables you to act as if you are afraid, and so you are saved from exposure to high levels of fear. This is psychic defense, but not in the Freudian manner that requires significant expenditure of psychic energy (e.g., repression). Instead, this weak theory can anticipate fear and can develop strategies for dealing with fear at a distance, so that in everyday life, the affect itself is rarely activated or experienced. If the individual encounters a situation that disrupts the quotidian functioning of a weak fear theory (a car going too fast, careening from one side of the street to the other), he may experience fear or perhaps panic. But Tomkins does not see this intense affect as "breaking through" unconscious defenses. Rather, this "fear which now overwhelms is . . . peculiar to this situation in which new threats have appeared" (2:321).

While Tomkins distinguishes between a finite number of affect models (monopolistic, intrusive, competitive, integrative) and four kinds of developmental analogs for those models (snowball, iceberg, coexistence, late bloomer), the taxonomic structures he describes are labile. Indeed, Tomkins is most interested in the ways our affect theories are dynamic and changeable: **"every theory, weak or strong, is in a relatively** unstable equilibrium, which is constantly shifting" (2:421). A strong theory, for example, is built through endless processes of construction, destruction, and reconstruction:

> The key to monopolism, as we define it, is not the existence of an organization which has attained an absolute level of strength. . . . It is our assumption that personality structure is continually changing. The monopolistic organization is also changing, but is one in which the change is in the same direction, continually reinterpreting in terms of the past what might have been seen as novelty, continually improving strategies which have broken down, so that they become more and more effective but which break down again and are again improved. (2:422)

The individual burdened by a monopolistic affect theory is caught in a distressing scramble to mobilize psychic strategies in the face of overwhelming affective traffic but then finds that those defenses disintegrate, and she is exposed, despite her best efforts, to toxic levels of negative affect.

Perhaps what is most interesting in Tomkins's account of affect theories, then, is not the capacity for integration or mutual accommodation (which he passes over fairly quickly) but how affect theories are built on discontinuity. Even in relatively benign circumstances, Tomkins argues, "discontinuities between perception, cognition, affect and action are the rule and not the exception" (2:372). It is this oscillation between the importance of skilled defenses against negative affects, on one hand, and the breakdown of those defenses, on the other, that is at the heart of Tomkins's account of an affect theory. Here, we think, lies one of the most intriguing challenges that Tomkins's work presents to the kinds of affect theorizing that tend to unilaterally favor flux over stasis or process over organization. Rather than arguing for static personality structures (as many of his psychological contemporaries did under the names *trait* or *temperament*) or for infinitely multiplying iterations of affective events, Tomkins gives us a model of theory building as construction, breakdown, renewal, and reassembly within a known number of parameters. It is this more algorithmic approach to both higher-order and individual theories that, we feel, amplifies the important and undertheorized middle ranges of affective agency. We pick up this notion again in the next two chapters (chapter 9, on scenes and scripts, and chapter 10, on ideology).

FURTHER READING

Tomkins's most extensive account of weak and strong (monopolistic) affect theories can be found in the final four chapters of *AIC2*: chapter 20, "Continuities and Discontinuities in the Impact of Humiliation: The Intrusion and Iceberg Models"; chapter 21, "Continuities and Discontinuities in the Impact of Humiliation: The Monopolistic and Snow Ball Models"; chapter 22, "The Structure of Monopolistic Humiliation Theory, Including the Paranoid Posture and Paranoid Schizophrenia"; and chapter 23, "Continuities and Discontinuities in the Impact of Humiliation: Some Specific Examples of the Paranoid Posture."

At the end of our opening paragraph, we are thinking of the work of Drew Westen *(The Political Brain)*, Lisa Blackman *(Immaterial Bodies)*, and Sianne Ngai *(Ugly Feelings)*.

For lively, recent engagements with Tomkins's notion of weak theory in modernist studies, see the special issue of *Modernism/Modernity* (September 2018) edited by Paul Saint-Amour and the many responses on that journal's Print Plus platform.

Eve Kosofsky Sedgwick has provided some preliminary clues about how to use the rubrics of weak and strong theory in the critical humanities in "Paranoid Reading and Reparative Reading; or, You're So Paranoid, You Probably Think This Introduction Is about You," and she makes a case for the non-oedipal, middle ranges of agency ("the notion that you can be relatively empowered or disempowered without annihilating someone else or being annihilated, or even castrating or being castrated" [632]) in "Melanie Klein and the Difference Affect Makes." On this latter argument about the middle ranges of affect, see Adam Frank, "Some Avenues for Feeling" and "Some Affective Bases for Guilt."

9
SCENES AND SCRIPTS

No small part of the pleasure of reading *AIC* comes from Tomkins's use of scenes, vignettes, and dialogue to illustrate his theoretical arguments. These theatrical forms, scattered especially over the second volume of *AIC,* are a significant aspect of his writing style (as are his lists). Consider, for example, the section titled "Production of a Total Affect-Shame Bind by Apparently Innocuous and Well-Intentioned Parental Action" (2:228), which begins, "Our hero is a child who is destined to have every affect totally bound by shame." Over two pages, Tomkins sketches an excruciating set of hypothetical scenes that take place around a 1950s American dinner table in which a child is shamed by his parents for expressing each of the primary affects: "Don't ever make that face again at the table—it's disgusting" (2:229), "Oh Robert, you'd think you hadn't eaten in a week, really!" (2:229), "Robert, where are your manners? Sit up" (2:229–30), "Robert, you could be a little more attentive, you don't have to sit there like a bump on a log. Say something" (2:230). Descriptions of childhood scenes animate Tomkins's writing ("On the playground, insult and counter-insult between peers is a commonplace: 'Oh yeah!' 'Yeah!' can be repeated endlessly, with the hostile sneer thrown back and forth as though it were a ball" [2:250]), while bits of invented dialogue demonstrate how affect theories are not only expressed and communicated but also taught and learned. In one instance, Tomkins offers a long, Tennessee Williams–style monologue to illustrate how a monopolistic humiliation theory can be created in a child through "verbal amplification." "You will be the death of me. You're no good—just like all children," it begins, and ends, a dozen or more lines later, with "God knows I try—but what good does it do? It's the same thing over and over again with you. You're hopeless" (2:399).

Clearly Tomkins's commitment to theatrical form was strong. He graduated from the University of Pennsylvania in 1930 with a concentration in playwriting and wrote the following in a letter to his colleague Irving Alexander almost forty years later: "For years, I have tried to express myself in playwriting and what I now realize is that any incapacity arises from over abstractness—I wish to prove a hypothesis—and in a sense am unwilling to immerse myself in the concrete details and lives of others sufficiently to give the play body" ("Silvan S. Tomkins," 251). According to Alexander, "psychology would provide that union of specificity and generality" (252) that Tomkins was searching for, but we would observe that only a highly dramaturgic model of psychology would satisfy: in *script theory,* Tomkins's general theory of personality that emerged late in his career, drama serves as a vital conceptual framework. Not long after retiring, Tomkins published "Script Theory: Differential Magnification of Affects" (1979). He would revise this, as well as a handful of related essays of the 1980s, for inclusion in *AIC3.* Script theory amends and elaborates the ideas of affect theory and development he explored thirty years earlier in *AIC2* (see chapter 8) and offers a late integration of many aspects of Tomkins's thinking.

Script theory distinguishes the scene, "a happening with a perceived beginning and end," from the script, "the individual's rules for predicting, interpreting, responding to, and controlling a magnified set of scenes" (3:83). The scene as a basic unit of experience "includes at least one affect and at least one object of that affect" (3:74) and thus always features *affective amplification.* Scripts, by contrast, are characterized by what Tomkins calls *psychological magnification,* "the phenomenon of connecting one affect-laden scene with another affect-laden scene. **Psychological magnification necessarily presupposes affective amplification of sets of connected scenes, but the affective amplification of a single scene does not necessarily lead to the psychological magnification of interconnected scenes**" (3:75). Recall that affective amplification makes an experience urgent: an infant's hunger, amplified by distress, urges a caregiver to feed her. Psychological magnification, a more sophisticated cognitive process, requires memory and the capacity to perceive similarity. Psychological magnification lets the child begin to order, interpret, or produce affective experiences. Scripts that organize scenes comprise aspects of the child's emerging personality. For example, the child who learns that his mother will appear when he cries from hunger has begun the process of script formation. That same child may learn to cry when he seeks attention or comfort from his mother for other reasons.

Not all scenes are magnified and embedded in scripts. What Tomkins calls transient scenes "may be highly amplified by affect but . . . remain isolated in the experience of the individual" (3:75). Being startled by a car horn, accidentally cutting oneself shaving, laughing at a joke—these experiences may be relatively isolated: "Lives are made up of large numbers of transient scenes. All experience is not necessarily interconnected with all other experience" (3:75). Tomkins also contrasts magnified scenes with habitual scenes, such as tying your shoelaces, crossing the street, or having breakfast with your spouse or partner. Habitual scenes, guided by what Tomkins, thirty years earlier, had called weak affect theories (see chapter 8), "do not become magnified, just because they are effective in achieving precisely what the individual intends they should achieve" (3:76). Note, the child learning to tie her shoes or cross the street, or the couple who have recently moved in together may initially experience considerable affect in these scenes (frustration, fear, joy). When they become habitual, the affect in these scenes fade. As Tomkins puts it, **the price of skill is the loss of the experience of value**" (3:76), an alternative description of what is more usually understood in terms of desire fueled by lack ("A husband and wife who become too skilled in knowing each other can enter the same valley of perceptual skill and become hardly aware of each other" [3:76]). Habitual scenes, however, can be magnified if circumstances change. An unexpected challenge to a marriage can return a couple to a renewed appreciation of and enjoyment in each other, just as a busy, confusing intersection can make us fearfully aware of the danger of street crossing.

Perhaps what is most useful about Tomkins's approach to scenes and scripts is its treatment of the multiple temporalities and spatialities of experience and its sophisticated understanding of how meaning itself emerges from the Proustian composition of memory, feeling, time, and place. Initially, for the very young infant who cannot associate scenes separated by intervals of time, almost all scenes are transient. Eventually, with sufficient cognitive and emotional development, "scenes experienced before can be coassembled with scenes presently experienced, together with scenes which are anticipated in the future. The present moment is embedded in the intersect between the past and the future in a central assembly via a constructive process we have called coassembly" (3:80). The concept of coassembly indexes Tomkins's basic structuralist commitment to combinatorial possibilities. He immediately offers a linguistic analogy: just as "the meaning of any one word is enriched and magnified by sequentially coassembling it with words which precede it and which follow it. So, too, is the meaning and impact of one affect-laden scene enriched and magnified by coassembling and relating it to another affect-laden scene" (3:80). But to this spatialized, structuralist understanding (for which scenes are like words, scripts like sentences that order, select, and organize words into greater units of meaning), Tomkins brings a Jamesian emphasis on the dynamics of temporal perception in the specious present. He puts it this way in a chapter on anger: "**The present scene as experienced is never a razor's edge.** It has extension in time through recruited memory of the immediate as well as remote past, through anticipation into the immediate and remote future, and through perception into the continuing, expanding present, which includes one's own as well as the other's responses, affective and motor, to the angering stimulus" (3:161).

We can gain some understanding of how scripts determine meaning by considering the psychological magnification of a transient scene. Suppose that a person who cuts himself shaving responds not only with distress but also with self-contempt: "What an idiot I am!" Suppose further that contempt already features in a group of scenes characterized by a perceived failure of attention in himself or others. What might be a transient scene is instead recruited to support a magnified grouping of scenes organized as a punitive contempt script: cutting oneself shaving becomes a failure of vigilance with damaging consequences that could or should have been avoided with proper, virtuous care. Another example: a momentary attraction to a passing stranger may be transient, an awareness of a pull of desire that emerges briefly into, then fades out of, consciousness. Or, such a scene can be magnified by and embedded in any number of different scripts: flirtation, seduction, aggression, inhibition, regret, and so on. An individual may have several scripts available to organize, interpret, or navigate such scenes of attraction, scripts that select for different contexts (a flirtation script in a coffee shop, a seduction script at a nightclub, an inhibition script at the workplace) or that are conjured up based on characteristics of the attractive person (hair color or texture, gait or manner of speaking).

For Tomkins, script theory offers a way to think about the complexity of experience insofar as it is at once determined and indeterminate. **"The effect of any set of scenes is indeterminate until the future either magnifies or attenuates such experience"** (3:87), he asserts, evoking something similar to what Freud called *Nachträglichkeit* (and what Laplanche has translated as *afterwardness*), the fundamental openness of the past to reinterpretation and redescription. Tomkins uses a different term in emphasizing the openness and multiplicity of the present: "the consequence of any experience is not singular but plural. **There is no single effect, but rather there are many effects, which change in time—what I have called the principle of plurideterminacy"** (3:87). Tomkins's definition of this principle is indebted to the mathematical analysis of circular causal systems in cybernetics:

> I have conceptualized differential magnification as a special case of plurideterminacy, which is the continuing change in causal status of any "cause" by the variation of conditions (including its "effects") which succeed it and embed it in the nexus of a connected system, not excluding anticipations of possibilities in the future which can and do either further magnify and/or attenuate different features of the origins of any scripted set of scenes. (3:83)

When his language reaches the limits of intelligibility, as it does here, Tomkins turns to mathematics. His formula for magnification advantage expresses in quantified terms what he had previously described in the qualitative terms of weak and strong affect theories. (In his reformulation, high magnification advantage is like strong theory, low magnification advantage like weak theory.) We encourage mathematically minded readers to pursue the details of Tomkins's discussions (3:80–83, 89–95), with this proviso: reading his computational approach to the perception of scenes and the ordering of scenes into scripts, it can seem as if Tomkins is waiting for his computer programmer to show up. Meanwhile, he is using his own amateur coding skills to sketch out the complex flows that he would like to formalize.

Tomkins's list of the general features of scripts (3:84–86) calls to mind his early thought experiment about what would be required to create an authentically humanlike artificial intelligence (see chapter 4). Such features of scripts, Tomkins implies, should guide engineers who are interested in creating machines with genuine personalities. We offer a brief summary of his list:

> Scripts are sets of ordering rules for the interpretation, evaluation, prediction, production, or control of scenes.
>
> Scripts are selective, incomplete, and varyingly accurate and inaccurate.
>
> Scripts are continually reordered and changed.
>
> Interscripts navigate between competing scripts.
>
> Scripts are more self-validating than self-fulfilling.
>
> Because they are incomplete, scripts require auxiliary augmentation from media mechanisms (the senses, language), theories, plots, maps, and other scripts.
>
> Scripts are modular (combinable and decomposable) and can be partitioned or split.

Tomkins's efforts to render experience in computational terms should not dissuade scholars in the humanities or social sciences from using the rich descriptive resources of script theory to differentiate affective practices across personalities, cultures, or peoples. When teaching Tomkins's script theory in Canada, for example, one of us (A.F.) uses the everyday example of a politeness script. It is typical for Canadian pedestrians to apologize not only when they bump into another pedestrian but when someone bumps into them. The automatic, rapidly uttered "sorry" can be considered a skilled, habitual (i.e., low magnification advantage) anger management script that serves to deflect conflict. (Driving, such politeness scripts go out the window.) Tomkins wanted script theory to serve as a bridge between individual psychology and "more general social science" (3:84): "what sociologists have called the definition of the situation and what I am defining as the script is to some extent the same phenomenon viewed from two different but related theoretical perspectives"

(3:84). Indeed, Tomkins's theory lets us think about how individuals inherit and transform scripts from their families, educational and media institutions, regions, nations, religions, and so on, and how, at the same time, a given social group can pick up and transform effective or compelling scripts that are created by individuals in that group. Script theory appears to us to be a useful hinge concept for moving between psychological and sociological perspectives.

The bulk of Tomkins's writing in *AIC3* focuses on the affects of anger and fear, describing in more or less detail a variety of scripts including what he calls ideologies, anger-management and anger-control scripts, damage-repair, limitation-remediation, decontamination, antitoxic, avoidance, change-review, power-recasting, affluence scripts, and others. It is, as usual, not possible to summarize Tomkins's discussions here. To give a reader a quick sense of the resources of this writing, consider Tomkins's description of affect control scripts, which govern the consciousness of affect; or the density, display, expression, and communication of affect; or the consequences, conditionality, and specificity of affect (3:262–65). We see, once again, the role of bits of actual dialogue in script theory: "'Enough is enough'; 'Simmer down'; 'You always cry at the least little thing'; 'You're too emotional' are protoypic affect-density-control scripts" (3:263), asserts Tomkins, who also offers examples of script rules for affect display and expression ("Wipe that smile off your face," "I don't want to hear any more whining," etc.). Any parent who, when reprimanding her child, has been surprised to hear her own parents' words come out of her mouth should have a fairly immediate and intuitive grasp of this aspect of script theory. Or consider Tomkins's chapter on "anger-driven power and recasting scripts" (3:458–70), in which a scene is recast with the positions of power reversed, for example, a child who frowns, says "no," and slaps a parent's hand reaching for a cookie. Here Tomkins seeks to rethink the psychoanalytic "theory of interiorization of good and bad objects" (3:458): "It is not necessarily a superego, ego ideal, or bad or good object which is interiorized but rather a specific simulation of how the other responded to the self—in this case via face, voice and hands—which is transformed in the recasting scene" (3:462). In such scenes, "the other is as salient as the self" (3:459), and it is the unity of the experienced scene that permits roles to be recast.

Another example of such reinterpretation of psychoanalytic dynamics or ideas is Tomkins's notion of nuclear scripts, "the scripts which must continue to grow in intensity of affect, of duration of affect, and in the interconnectedness of scenes via the conjoint promise of endless, infinite, unconditional ends" (3:95). These scripts organize "the good scenes we can never totally or permanently achieve or possess" (3:95) as well as the bad scenes we cannot avoid or master; that is, they organize scenes of oedipal desire and our encounters with death. "The male child who loves his mother excessively," asserts Tomkins, "can neither totally possess her (given an unwanted rival) nor totally renounce her. He is often destined, however, to keep trying and, characteristically, to keep failing" (3:96). Given his commitment to the principle of plurideterminacy, it may surprise some readers to encounter the language of "destiny" here. It does appear that his conception of nuclear scripts undermines his urge, so often expressed elsewhere in his writing, to find alternatives to Freud's developmental framework, as he puts it in *AIC4*: "In contrast to Freud's vision of civilization and its inherently tragic discontents, [script theory] is a vision of the equally inherent but less essentially tragic consequences of the differential magnification of a very rich set of potentialities for human civilizations" (4:26). There is no doubt that Tomkins's theory is open to an enriched and more varied set of possible developmental outcomes than is classical psychoanalytic theory. Nevertheless, it still raises the question of the inevitability of some forms of human experience. By no means does it resolve this question.

FURTHER READING

Our discussion is largely a summary of "Affect and Cognition: Cognition as Central and Causal in Psychological Magnification," chapter 3 of *AIC3*. Note that we have set aside Tomkins's definition of "plot" ("the whole connected set of scenes lived in sequence is called the *plot* of a life" [3:83]), which neglects the usual association of plot with narrative cause and effect. As far as we can tell, the notion of plot does not play a significant role in Tomkins's script theory. Elsewhere in *AIC3*, Tomkins explores many classes of scripts. Readers interested in reading more about nuclear scripts in particular will wish to examine the case studies of Sculptor in which Tomkins engages in self-analysis.

We also consulted, in *AIC4,* "Cognition: What Is It and Where Is It?" (chapter 2) as well as *Exploring Affect,* part IV, especially the section titled "Revisions in Script Theory—1990," in which Tomkins maps a set of salient scripts back onto his theory of primary affects. For more on script theory, see Tomkins's "Script Theory: Differential Magnification of Affects" (1979), "Script Theory" (1987), and "Scripting the Macho Man" (1988). See also Virginia Demos's detailed clinical notes on Tomkins's script theory in *The Affect Theory of Silvan Tomkins for Psychoanalysis and Psychotherapy* (chapters 6 and 8).

10
IDEOLOGY

Tomkins is interested in the affective infrastructure of ideology: What are the affects that orient individuals or societies toward particular ideologies? And how do the ideologies of individuals and the formal ideologies that govern societies resonate with and reinforce each other? Tomkins defines ideology as **"any organized set of ideas about which human beings are at once most articulate and most passionate, and for which there is no evidence and about which they are least certain"** ("Affect and the Psychology of Knowledge," 73). He thinks of ideology, then, not simply as a cognitive creed or a sociopolitical standpoint or an economic effect; it is also an affectively structured stance. Ideology materializes from the social traffic in affects *and* from the particular socialization of affects that have scripted individual lives (more of which later). We think that Tomkins's framework for thinking about ideology might be invigorating for the current critical scene. Because it attempts to integrate personological approaches (in-depth understandings of the personality of a specific individual; see chapter 11) and those knowledges that foreground social norms, networks of power, social stratification, or discursive regimes, Tomkins's work on ideology offers some hitherto underutilized tools for thinking about the dynamics of sociopsychic formation.

Tomkins's work on affect and ideology is part what he calls "the psychology of knowledge" (see chapter 13). An analog of the sociology of knowledge, the psychology of knowledge is concerned with "the ebb and flow of affect investment in ideas and ideology, in methods and styles of investigation, and in what is considered acceptable criteria of evidence" ("Affect and the Psychology of Knowledge," 73). Reviewing a huge literature of controversies in metaphysics, mathematics, the philosophy of science, epistemology, jurisprudence, aesthetics, political theory, educational theory, psychiatry, and psychology, Tomkins finds a persistent ideological bifurcation in these fields. He argues that these intellectual disputes orient either toward a *humanistic* pole or toward a *normative* one. Humanistic ideologies idealize the human being as "an active, creative, thinking, desiring, loving force of nature" (3:26), whereas in normative ideologies, the human being is fully realized "only through struggle toward, participation in, and conformity to a norm" (3:26). That is, irrespective of the content of a particular dispute (mathematical or legal or political or psychiatric), knowledges tend to be structured according to a consistent, recognizable ideological *polarity*: humanistic–normative (or left–right). This ideological polarity is structured by affective concerns:

> the humanistic position is the one that attempts to maximize positive affect for the individual and for all of his interpersonal relationships. In contrast, the normative position is that norm compliance is the primary value and that positive affect is a *consequence* of norm compliance but not to be directly sought as a goal. Indeed, the suffering of negative affect is assumed to be a frequent experience and an inevitable consequence of the human condition. (3:28)

It is perhaps unexpected that Tomkins thinks of ideology in terms of a polarity, given his allegiance elsewhere to theories of multiple, co-assembling affects and his interest in interdependencies between the various components of a psychological system (affects with cognitions with drives with socialization scripts with neurological firing). Indeed, Irving Alexander (Tomkins's student, collaborator, and friend) worries that such an approach is uncharacteristic of Tomkins's work:

> When I reflect on the content of his contribution to ideology, I am struck by one feature that seems not at all typical of the way he worked: to cast things in a binary framework or to treat them in a typological fashion. In this instance, I am referring to his dichotomization of the right and the left wing. ("Ideology," 105)

We argue that the uses of polarity are different, in Tomkins's hands, from the more rigid structures and cleavages of binaries that Alexander identifies. The sense of oppositionality and exclusion that is baked into the definition of a binary is leavened by the magnetic, chemical, and biological senses of "polarity" as *a tendency to orient.* What we see at the core of Tomkins's work on ideology, then, is not a division of psyches and societies into two distinct and exclusive types (humanistic vs. normative; left vs. right) but a thick description of the scripts, histories of socialization, and resonances that join individuals, affects, and societies.

Indeed, Tomkins first outlines his account of ideology ("Left and Right: A Basic Dimension of Ideology and Personality") in a book of essays in honor of Henry Murray, his mentor at the Harvard Psychological Clinic. It was at the clinic that Tomkins was first introduced to Murray's "personology": a way of thinking about personality that was concerned with understanding specific individuals through a variety of overlapping measures (psychoanalytic, biographical, physiological, behavioral, observational, statistical) (see chapter 11). It seems to us that Tomkins's account of ideology is more indebted to the vicissitudes of personology than it is to the strictures of binarized thinking.

This understanding of polarity as a general orientation rather than a forced choice is formalized in the instructions for Tomkins's Polarity Scale—a little used and curious tool for assessing an individual's ideology. The scale presents subjects with a series of paired items, for example,

Numbers were invented/Numbers were discovered

The mind is more like a lamp which illuminates whatever it shines on/The mind is like a mirror which reflects whatever it strikes

It is disgusting to see an adult cry/It is distressing to see an adult cry

Rather than require that test subjects choose one item in the pair over the other, the Polarity Scale gives subjects a number of ways to respond: "Consider each of the following 59 pairs of ideas and check which of them you agree with. If you agree with both of them check both of them. If you agree with neither do not check either one." That is, Tomkins's pairs are not dichotomized alternatives; they are prompts to be pondered and interpreted in a more open-ended fashion. The scale allows a subject to breach the law of noncontradiction and claim, for example, that numbers were both discovered *and* invented. The middle has been asserted rather than excluded. In fact, Tomkins argues that the middle of the road can be a radical ideology rather than a weak or compromising stance (see chapter 13). It is not clear to us, then, that Tomkins's key concern in his ideology theory is simply "the incompatibility of the two value positions [humanistic/normative]," as Alexander claims ("Ideology," 105). His theory of ideology puts in place a distinction, not to consolidate oppositions, but seemingly to—once again—build a system in which the components might have multiple degrees of freedom to link and delink. The dynamic and interconnected nature of ideologies becomes more evident in Tomkins's account of how individual postures coassemble with social formations. He argues that ideologies are predicated on *ideo-affective postures*. An ideo-affective posture is "any loosely organized set of feelings and ideas about feelings" ("Left and Right," 74). An authoritarian attitude would be an example of an ideo-affective posture: children should be firmly disciplined; familiarity breeds contempt; those who break the law should always be punished for the good of society. All individuals have ideo-affective postures, Tomkins argues, but not all individuals have an ideology ("a highly organized and articulate set of ideas about anything" [74]), for example, a clear set of guidelines about how to regulate the behavior of children in educational settings. What is interesting, for Tomkins, is how the more loosely structured beliefs and feelings of our ideo-affective postures are engaged by ideology and how (when they are sufficiently alike) they resonate with, reinforce, and strengthen each other. Ideologies are most compelling when they are closely aligned with an affective infrastructure: "The distinction which we have drawn between the basic ideo-affective postures and ideology proper is a fundamental one, and societies can and do die when their ideologies atrophy through increasing irrelevance to the changing ideo-affective postures" (78).

Two key questions emerge for Tomkins: How are ideo-affective postures fashioned through the socialization of affects in childhood? What is the relationship between such ideo-affective postures and the more highly structured ideological positions we might adopt as individuals or societies? Take, for example, the socialization of distress. When a child cries, the parent (following her own ideo-affective postures and ideological commitments) may either soothe the child (picking the child up, perhaps converting negative affect into a rewarding scene) or may attempt to fight the distress, demanding that the child suppress his response ("If you don't stop crying, I will give you something to really cry about"

[3:27]). What is generated in such scenes is a particular ideo-affective orientation in the child that will have broader ideological significance:

If the child internalizes his parent's ideo-affective posture and his ideology, he has learned a very basic posture toward suffering, which will have important consequences for resonance to ideological beliefs quite remote from the nursery and the home. (3:27)

A similar case is true for anger. In two remarkable chapters on ideology and the socialization of anger, Tomkins outlines the various ways in which anger can be socialized punitively (where the child is taught to control anger but not to modulate or tolerate it) or in a more rewarding fashion (where the child is taught to cope with the sources, experiences, and outcomes of anger). In both cases, the child is being prepared for "ideological partnership according to the predominant ideologies of his nation, class, ethnic[ity], gender, and religion, as well as the idiosyncratic biases of his parents" (3:216).

This socialization of affects does not operate in a singular fashion to determine an ideo-affective posture. Rather, the differential socialization of distress or anger is amplified by the differential socialization of the other affects, in this and other scenes. Nor does Tomkins limit the meaning of socialization to the unilateral effects of parental behavior on a child:

Instead of describing a socialization of anger as involving physical punishment for a display of anger or aggression, we would include both the sequence of interactions which led up to such punishment and, most critically, the immediate and delayed responses by the *child* to the punishment, as well as the further responses of the parent to the child's responses. (3:218–19)

That is, ideo-affective postures (or what he will later call scripts; see chapter 9) emerge out of a sequence of affectively intense scenes that are experienced in quite specific ways. Tomkins argues that three things must happen in relation to such scenes for them to become ideologically consequential: the child must hear the parent express a certain ideology, the child must also see these words translated into action, and the child must see the affect frequently displayed on the parent's face. For example, in the punitive socialization of disgust, the child "hears the parents frequently expound an ideology that asserts the worthlessness of man" (2:351). The child also sees the parents act in a way that is consistent with these ideologies. Here Tomkins has a devastating inventory of parental disdain:

> Stray animals are thrown out of the house if they are brought into the house by the child. The friends of the child are derogated, and he is asked not to entertain them at home nor to visit them, since their parents are contemptible or suspect. Minority groups are discriminated against, and the parents express satisfaction whenever life becomes harder for them. Underdeveloped nations, disaster areas, appeals for help in the fight against disease, these and numerous other appeals for time, money and energy are ostentatiously and piously declined. Civic and other duties are declined on the ground that they are not worthy of support. (2:352)

And finally, the child must see the parent display disgust: "belief and action require the amplification by [parental] affective display to entirely capture the imagination of the child" (2:307). It is the confluence of ideology, action, and affect that will establish the child's ideo-affective posture, and this in turn will likely resonate strongly with a wider set of ideological positions available in the child's world.

FURTHER READING

Tomkins first outlines his theory of ideology in "Left and Right: A Basic Dimension of Ideology and Personality," and he discusses ideology and anger scripts at length in chapter 8 of *AIC3* ("Ideology and Anger"). If readers are interested in an example of how Tomkins's work on ideology has been used in empirical contexts, we refer them to Rae Carlson and Julia Brincka's study of the ideological and gendered scripts governing subjects' perceptions of candidates (Reagan, Bush, Mondale, Ferraro) in the 1984 U.S. presidential election ("Studies in Script Theory: III. Ideology and Political Imagination"). This study is structured by an ideo-affective preference for the middle ground.

The Polarity Scale was published by Springer in 1964, and Tomkins gives a detailed account of the origins of and uses for the scale in "Affect and the Psychology of Knowledge." Nonetheless, the scale has not been widely used in the social science literatures. For some examples of its use, see Marjaana Lindeman and Minna Sirelius on food choice ideologies ("Food Choice Ideologies: The Modern Manifestations of Normative and Humanist Views of the World"); Donald Mosher and James Sullivan's formulation of a modified Polarity Scale ("Sexual Polarity Scale"); and Vicki Ashton and James Dwyer's correlation of ideology and left–right laterality in the body ("The Left: Lateral Eye Movements and Ideology"). Virginia Demos discusses the ongoing usefulness of Tomkins's polarity theory in *The Affect Theory of Silvan Tomkins for Psychoanalysis and Psychotherapy* (154–62).

INTERLUDE
TOMKINS AND DARWIN

There is a genealogical shorthand in critical, clinical, and empirical literatures that links Silvan Tomkins very directly to Charles Darwin. It has become common for researchers, as a way of introducing Tomkins's affect theory, to claim that this work *follows* Darwin, *builds* or *expands* on Darwin, *derives* from or *revivifies* Darwin's 1872 account of emotion in *The Expression of the Emotions in Man and Animals*. Sometimes these small gestures of provenance point to a Darwinian lineage or tradition for which Tomkins is alleged to be the contemporary standard-bearer. Donald Nathanson, for example, speaks of "the red thread that stretches from Darwin to Tomkins" (30), and Melissa Gregg and Gregory Seigworth suggest that "with Tomkins, affect follows a quasi-Darwinian 'innate-ist' bent toward matters of evolutionary hardwiring" (5).

We feel that the presupposition that Tomkins is very much like Darwin, or that he can be rendered taxonomically cognate with Darwin, requires some elaboration and revision. Such assertions tend to under-read the dynamism and innovation of Darwin's work on emotion, and they can imply that Tomkins's work is more universalist or biologically concrete than it is. For example, the neuroscientist Joseph LeDoux, using a fairly conventional appraisal of Darwin, positions Tomkins's work in ways that are, quite simply, incorrect: "Building on Darwin, Tomkins proposed that several *primary* (or *basic*) *emotions* are genetically built into the human brain by natural selection and expressed identically in everyone regardless of race or cultural background. . . . Like Darwin, Tomkins focused on universal expressions" (121). We have disputed readings of Tomkins as determinist or universalist in earlier chapters (chapters 3 and 4). It seems to us that some of these misrepresentations of Tomkins's work can be attributed to how the relationship between Tomkins and Darwin has been framed, and it is that framing that we address here.

In the first interlude, we made the claim that there are connections between Tomkins and Spinoza that have been overlooked and that there is benefit in thinking about these two bodies of work together. In this interlude, we move contrariwise, arguing that perhaps too much has been made, or assumed, about the alliance between Darwin and Tomkins. In these interludes, we hope to complicate the easy division of literatures on emotion into clearly defined, and clearly distinct, Spinozist (Continental) or Darwinian (Anglo-American) traditions. Without doubt, important textual similarities link Tomkins to Darwin. We wonder, for example, if Tomkins's decision to give the primary affects joint names that express the affect at both low and high intensity (e.g., interest-excitement, fear-terror, anger-rage) might be influenced in part by Darwin's strategy of ordering his material in *The Expression of the Emotions in Man and Animals* according to families of emotional responses (e.g., chapter 11 is named "Disdain-Contempt-Disgust-Guilt-Pride, Etc.-Helplessness-Patience-Affirmation and Negation"). In addition, we note that both writers are skilled users of anecdotal and biographical data. Nonetheless, it is our argument that Tomkins's ties to Darwin are not as intellectually, or indeed affectively, intense as his ties to the psychological theories of Sigmund Freud and Henry Murray (see chapter 11). As Tomkins himself notes in a late paper that reviews the study of personality,

> Darwin's theory of evolution was magnificent, but it lacked the genetic infrastructure supplied by Mendel, and lacked the helix model of Crick and Watson. What shall we do to revitalize the study of personality? Should we look for the helix, or for the evolutionary sweep, or something in between? I would suggest that one vital clue to our problem is to be found in Freud. ("The Rise, Fall, and Resurrection," 447–48)

We claim, then, not that Darwin and Tomkins are detached from each other but that the influence of the former on the latter ought to be more carefully specified.

In the first instance, it is clear from even a cursory reading of *AIC* and some of Tomkins's more widely circulated papers ("What and Where Are the Primary Affects?," "The Quest for Primary Motives") that his relation to Darwin is more attenuated and less deferential than one might first presume: reference to Darwin is not present in those places where one might most expect to find it; even when Tomkins does turn to Darwin, his use of that work is usually fairly brief; and his tone toward Darwin is often one of mild rebuke. For example, in a chapter on evolution and affect (where one might anticipate frequent use of Darwin's writing on emotion), Tomkins is actually most interested in the work of two much less prominent twentieth-century researchers. The first of these is the surgeon George Washington Crile, who argued that different animal species have different profiles of arousal, maintenance, and decline of the same affect. The second is the biologist Curt Richter, whose experiments with Norwegian rats showed how selection for specific affects and their bodily correlates (e.g., fear) is different in the domesticated and wild types of the species. Having discussed this work, Tomkins's central claim about evolution and the affects then proceeds without direct reference to Darwin at all:

> If man can selectively breed other animals for such specific affective and behavioral characteristics as social responsiveness, aggressiveness, individualism, flexibility, emotionality and maze running ability, despite his ignorance of the specific genetic factors which are involved, it is certainly possible that natural selection, through differential reproductive success, could also have favored specific affective characteristics in man. It is our belief that such was indeed the case and that **natural selection has operated on man to heighten three distinct classes of affect—affect for the preservation of life, affect for people and affect for novelty.** (1:169)

Similarly, in a chapter on the face, Tomkins refers to *The Expression of the Emotions in Man and Animals* only in passing. Instead, he engages with a wide variety of clinical and empirical research in psychology, psychoanalysis, and physiology. Tomkins's most sustained engagement with evolutionary argument in this chapter is in relation to Duchenne's *Mechanism of Human Facial Expression* (1862) and the work of an early twentieth-century anatomist Ernst Huber. Their work provides a frame not just for Tomkins to think about the "possible relations between specific facial muscles and specific affects" (1:204) but also to make one of the most consequential arguments in *AIC*: that "affect is primarily facial behavior" (1:204; see also chapter 2). That is, Tomkins departs from the idea (in Darwin) that the face is simply a site for the expression of emotions that have been generated elsewhere in the body and instead makes the claim that the face (and later, he argues, the skin) is the locus of affect. Quite specifically, in Tomkins's affect theory, it is the awareness of the feedback of facial responses that is the experience of affect (and this is part of Tomkins's relation to a Jamesian tradition). This kind of claim about the phenomenology of affect (how does it feel to be angry?) is not the same as Darwin's interest in the phylogenesis of rage (the furious snarl shared by man and animals). If Tomkins needs to put Darwin to one side to make one of the most important claims in *AIC,* and if Tomkins's use of evolutionary ideas seems oriented more toward mental states and the socialization of feelings than to the physiology of descent, then it becomes important to qualify how intellectually allied these two bodies of work really are.

Tomkins's most sustained use of Darwin comes, not in relation to a theory of evolution, but as he defines the primary affects. In the chapters that delineate each of the primary affects, Tomkins turns initially to Darwin to describe the bodily contours of that affect, but in each case, he quickly admonishes or revises Darwin's contribution. He notes, for example, that interest-excitement is missing from Darwin's classification of the emotions. In relation to fear, Tomkins notes that Darwin "properly includes autonomic and skin responses as well as motor responses" (3:495) in his description of fear (i.e., "trembling, the erection of hair, cold perspiration, pallor, widely opened eyes, the relaxation of most of the muscles, and by the whole body cowering down-ward, or held motionless" [*The Expression of the Emotions in Man and Animals,* 360–61]), but he also argues that this definition pays insufficient attention to the face. He claims that Darwin's definition of fear

> should also have included the cry of terror, the raising and drawing together of the eyebrows, the tensing of the lower eyelid as well as opening of the eyes, the stretching of the lips back as well as the opening of the mouth, and finally, the contraction of the platysma muscles of the neck in extreme terror. (3:495)

While Tomkins returns repeatedly to the intimacy between specific facial muscles and specific affects, his uses for evolution don't stop there. He is also interested in the social relations that the increasing visibility of primate facial musculature and expressiveness make possible. The human face "seems to have evolved in part as an organ for the maximal transmission of information, to the self and to others" ("What and Where Are the Primary Affects?," 120). That is, an account of the evolutionary fine-tuning of facial musculature and affect programs is not an end in itself for Tomkins. Rather, it is one means by which he is able to build an affect theory that is psychosocial in nature.

In his last public lecture Tomkins gives one of the most concise accounts of his relation to Darwin. There he repeats the claim from *AIC* that the face is where the affects are: "a smile is where it appears to be. It is not in a group of happy cortical neurons nor in the folds of the stomach" ("Inverse Archaeology," 284). He names this approach to affect an "inverse archeology," as it reverses the archeological trope that affects are deeply buried, fossilized events from the past. Darwin's focus on the *expression* of emotions is exemplary of the archeological tradition Tomkins wishes to invert:

> Darwin thought there was something being expressed. What he saw wasn't it. It was expressing something else. That is not inverse archeology. **Inverse archeology not only locates motivation on those surfaces where it appears to be, rather than somewhere else, which it represents and expresses, but it also says that facial affect is at once individual and private and social and shared nonverbal communication.** (285)

Following Tomkins on this point, we might say that he doesn't so much *follow* Darwin as he turns him *upside down* or *inside out*.

What is needed, if we are to deploy the conjunction Tomkins–Darwin, is a more expansive sense of the intellectual lineage that these two theorists are said to share. As a first gesture, we ought to be wary of the temptation to create a fixed intellectual and historical origin in 1872 with the publication of *The Expression of the Emotions in Man and Animals,* and we could pay more attention to the nineteenth-century work that immediately predates Darwin (and on which Tomkins sometimes draws): that of the neurologist Duchenne, the anatomists Pierre Gratiolet and Charles Bell, the psychiatrist James Crichton-Browne. Moving forward from 1872, we ought not to overlook the very interesting empirical work in the early twentieth century on facial recognition and the physiology of the face that likely came to Tomkins's attention. Maria Gendron and Lisa Feldman Barrett dispute the commonplace notion that there was a dark age in the study of emotion in the early twentieth century (instigated by behaviorism) that was finally lifted in the 1960s with work by Tomkins, among others:

> As it turns out, then, the "Dark Ages" of emotion in psychology were not really that dark after all. . . . The basic emotion perspective, usually traced back almost exclusively to Darwin, actually emerged more slowly with fundamental assumptions being articulated by theorists such as Dewey, Watson, Allport, and McDougall. (334–35)

Indeed, Tomkins ("Quest for Primary Motives") himself remarks on these historical precedents for his theories, noting the importance of the work of the physiologist Walter Cannon, the endocrinologist Hans Selye, the biologist Curt Richter, the psychologist Eckhard Hess, and the ethologist Konrad Lorenz, who were all publishing in the early to mid-twentieth century.

Similarly, Carroll Izard and Maurice Haynes sketch a brief history of empirical research on contempt to contest the presumption that there was very little in the way of research on emotion after Darwin and before Tomkins. They point us to a paper published by Jean Frois-Wittmann in the *Journal of Experimental Psychology* in 1930 that investigated how people make judgments about the facial expression of emotion. Showing 165 college students photographs of posed facial expressions, Frois-Wittmann found that these observers frequently agreed about what emotion they thought was being depicted. We note, in order to keep expanding and diversifying the intellectual network that enfolds Tomkins, that Frois-Wittmann (a cousin of Pierre Janet) returned to France after completing this work at Princeton University and became a psychoanalyst and a member of the Surrealist movement in Paris.

The more one follows the threads of citation in and around Tomkins's work, the less it appears that there is a direct line that ties him in a dutiful way to Darwin—or, indeed, to the West. Vinay Dharwadker has made a compelling (and meticulously argued) case that there are connections not simply between Darwin and Tomkins but also between both men's work and an eighteen-hundred-year-old Sanskrit text—Bharata's treatise on the performing arts, the *Nātyaśhāstra*. The interrelations of these texts on emotion, he argues, "are neither slight nor superficial" (1381).

Rather,

> the forty-nine stable emotional states, auxiliary emotions, and psychosomatic symptoms that Bharata classifies for the arts coincide in exquisite detail with most of the thirty-four emotions that Darwin, in his later years, maps out. . . . Moreover, Bharata's typology of eight stable emotional states that frame all secondary feelings and emotions interlocks firmly with Tomkins's hierarchy of nine primary affects. (1381)

Dharwadker neither conflates Darwin and Tomkins and Bharata nor places them in entirely different epistemological spheres. Instead, he is interested in how these texts meet, contradict, repeat, and reinvent each other. He finds particular resonance between Tomkins's cybernetic modeling of the relation between cognition and affect (partial independence, partial dependence, and partial interdependence) and how the *Nātyaśhāstra* models thinking and feeling as two modes of being in the world. Yet, he is also clear that the *bhavas* that Bharata describes (a term encompassing general states of being, both short and enduring emotional states, and certain bodily states) cannot be mapped onto the primary affects as Tomkins defines them. Dharwadker enmeshes these three theories of emotion in ways that confound simple linear models of temporal, cultural, and textual influence, helping us to further dissolve the easy calculus that connects Tomkins directly or exclusively to Darwin.

FURTHER READING

Darwin's *The Expression of the Emotions in Man and Animals,* published in 1872, is the place where Darwin gives his most sustained account of emotion. We refer readers initially to "What Is an Emotion?" and "The Place of Affectional Facts in a World of Pure Experience" if they wish to engage with William James's theory of emotion.

In terms of early twentieth-century theories of emotion, we recommend the work of the physiologist Walter Cannon (who, along with Philip Bard, argued for the role of thalamic and hypothalamic structures in the expression and experience of emotion). There is, of course, much to be said about the place of affect in Freud's work (see, e.g., André Green, *The Fabric of Affect in the Psychoanalytic Discourse*). The details of Jean Frois-Wittmann's psychoanalytic career after Princeton have been gleaned from Roudinesco. See Lisa Blackman's *Immaterial Bodies* for a genealogy of twentieth-century psychology that takes affect and the body to be central considerations.

PART III
CONSCIOUSNESS

11
PSYCHOANALYSIS AT THE HARVARD PSYCHOLOGICAL CLINIC

Tomkins began studying consciousness at a time when it had been subordinated by both behaviorism (in favor of observable action) and psychoanalysis (in favor of the unconscious). In the preface to the first volume of *AIC,* he remarks that his affect theory "is not primarily focused on what is current knowledge. I have sought to explore new territory. It is my intention to reopen issues which have long remained in disrepute in American Psychology: affect, imagery and consciousness" (1:vii). In part III, we survey the kinds of methods (personology, psychology of knowledge) and intellectual precedents (cybernetics, psychoanalysis) that shape Tomkins's account of consciousness, and we finish, where Tomkins finished, with his expansive understanding of the human being as a *minding system* built through the dynamic and changing co-assembly of affect and imagery and consciousness.

We begin with two anecdotes.

Story one. Gordon Allport, the American psychologist who pioneered quantitative research on personality, is en route from Constantinople to Cambridge, Massachusetts. It is 1920, and Allport is just twenty-two years old. He is returning from a teaching position in Constantinople to take up a fellowship at Harvard that will underwrite his graduate study in the relatively new discipline of psychology. He will go on to serve in the Department of Psychology at Harvard until his death in 1967. In 1920, Allport is stopping in Vienna to see his brother. He has also taken this trip as an opportunity to write to Sigmund Freud and ask for an appointment. And Freud has agreed to see him. Allport arrives at Freud's house and is ushered into his office: "He did not speak to me but sat in expectant silence, for me to state my mission. I was not prepared for silence and had to think fast to find a suitable conversational gambit" (*The Person in Psychology,* 383). Allport's conversational opening is a story about a small boy whom he had observed in the tram on the way to Freud's house. This boy seemed to have "a conspicuous dirt phobia. He kept saying to his mother, 'I don't want to sit there . . . don't let that dirty man sit beside me.' To him everything was *schmutzig*" (383). Freud listens to this story, fixes his "kindly therapeutic eyes" upon the socially anxious Allport, and asks, "And was that little boy you?" (383).

Story two. Sometime in late 1937 or early 1938, a month or two before the *Anschluss,* Henry Murray, the newly appointed director of the Harvard Psychological Clinic, meets Freud in Vienna. Murray reports that the invitation came from Freud himself and that as soon as he arrives at Berggasse 19, Freud asks why he (Freud) didn't get an honorary degree at the Harvard Tercentenary, whereas Jung did. Murray explains that the Department of Psychology had nominated four psychologists for this honorary degree, ranking Freud first, followed by Carl Jung, Pierre Janet, and Jean Piaget. Nonetheless, someone (perhaps Edwin Boring, the chair of the department) had decided that Freud would not be interested in this award, especially after the honorary degree bestowed by Clark University in 1909. Moreover, given the state of his health, it was felt that Freud would be unlikely to attend. Murray recalls that "we were told he'd never come; so we didn't invite him. And what did he care, a great man like that, and a little place in Cambridge, Mass?" ("Interview with Henry A. Murray," 324). After this explanation is provided to Freud, the two men move on to other matters: "We changed the topic right away. And we had a lot of things to say, interests in common. He showed me all around the room. We talked about Egyptians" (325).

The relation between academic psychology and psychoanalysis, particularly as it manifested in the parochial setting of Harvard University in the 1930s and 1940s, was formative for Tomkins's theorization of affect and consciousness. When Silvan Tomkins arrived at Harvard in 1935 as a postdoctoral fellow in philosophy, Allport and Murray were already well established as researchers in the Department of Psychology, and their various affiliations and disidentifications with Freud and Freudianism were entrenched. Within two years, Tomkins had transferred his position, and his affections, from philosophy to psychology. He took up a position at the Harvard Psychological Clinic in 1937, moving into an intellectual environment where the relevance of psychoanalysis to a newly institutionalized, disciplined, and Americanized psychology was being fiercely debated. Some faculty in the department vociferously rejected Freudianism. The behaviorist-turned-neurophysiologist Karl Lashley, for example, felt that the Freudian theory of libido had been postulated without regard for certain important physiological facts:

> The problem of motivation is far more complex than the Freudians would have us believe and its solution is to be sought in the investigation of many related fields: the analysis of specific instinctive responses, the neural basis of emotions, the mutual influence of habits, the total integration of all such systems of reaction. ("Physiological Analysis of the Libido," 202)

Allport built a theory of personality that borrowed from psychoanalysis but remained largely untouched by its more radical claims:

> I am now appropriating [the psychoanalytic term ego] to signify the recentering that is taking place in psychological theory. ("The Ego in Contemporary Psychology," 453)

Other faculty turned to psychoanalysis to treat significant personal issues but found it imperfect:

> Now, four years after the close of the analysis, I find myself quite uncertain as to whether it has made any important change in me. (Boring, 10)

While Murray was perhaps the most faithfully psychoanalytic of these Harvard men, his engagement with Freudianism was defiantly heterodox:

> Psychoanalysis stands for a conceptual system which explains, it seems to me, as much as any other. But this is no reason for going in blind and swallowing the whole indigestible bolus, cannibalistically devouring the totem father in the hope of acquiring his genius, his authoritative dominance, and thus rising to power in

the psychoanalytic society, that battle-ground of Little Corporals. No; I, for one, prefer to take what I please, suspend judgment, reject what I please, speak freely. ("What Should Psychologists Do about Psychoanalysis?," 157)

While being closest, personally and professionally, to Murray and to the psychological–psychoanalytic synthesis that Murray fostered under the name "personology" at the Harvard Psychological Clinic (**"My debt to Henry A. Murray is great. It was his work that turned me back to the study of psychology"** [*Thematic Apperception Test,* viii]), Tomkins nonetheless seems to have valued aspects of these other critiques of psychoanalysis that circulated around Cambridge. Like Lashley, Tomkins developed a capacious understanding of many different fields that might bear on the question of motivation. His friend and colleague Irving Alexander notes that in these early years at Harvard, Tomkins "read widely and mastered large literatures in psychology, an achievement which would become clearly evident in volume 1 of *Affect Imagery Consciousness*" ("Silvan S. Tomkins," 253). Like Allport, Tomkins felt that conscious motivations were important in understanding human psychology. Like Boring, he went into analysis, although Tomkins felt that his treatment was successful. While others might have been tempted, or coerced, into aligning themselves more fully with one or other of these intellectual camps, Tomkins seems to have taken in a number of very different critiques and uses of psychoanalysis, and he built a theory about the motivating influence of the affects that was independent of all these figures, even Murray.

Of course, beyond these internecine disputes about psychoanalysis, there were other scholars in Cambridge who had established emotion as an object of study well before Tomkins's arrival. William James's philosophy of emotion and Walter Cannon's studies of the neurophysiology of emotion must have been known to Tomkins, and as we have noted in earlier chapters (see chapter 2 and the interlude on Tomkins and Darwin), this work was influential on his theory of affect as it emerged in the decades following his time at Harvard.

Tomkins worked at the Harvard Psychological Clinic for a decade (from 1937 to 1947), a period he would later represent as his "golden years" (Alexander, "Silvan S. Tomkins," 253). His first publications from the clinic demonstrate a methodological approach to disciplinary psychological knowledge that would be amplified and intensified in his later work (i.e., critical but nonetheless deeply engaged and inquisitive).

These early publications were three papers, printed as a series in the *Journal of Psychology* in 1943, that report on the different kinds of verbal responses that subjects had to an electric shock that was administered when they made a mistake in a learning experiment: "reminded me of an electric chair"; "is this supposed to make me cautious?"; "I like the shocks"; "I'm scared, sweating all over"; "I'm sure I'm going to taste the shock this time"; "felt as if a shark or some animal were biting you"; "this experiment is stupid" ("An Analysis of the Use of Electric Shock," 287–88). One only has to listen to the responses of these subjects, Tomkins argued, to realize that **"an electric shock is all things to all men"** (285). At this time, with behaviorism in the ascendancy in U.S. psychology, the shock was taken to be a standard (psychologically uncomplicated) experimental stimulus that could be used to punish rat and human alike. Tomkins's interpretation of his data was a rethinking of this presumption. A classical learning paradigm that employs electric shock will elicit all manner of different reactions (fear, anxiety, pleasure, aggression, pride): "the shock probably always means something quite idiosyncratic which the subject rarely verbalizes and which the experimenter even less often understands" (288).

What seems important, in terms of thinking about Tomkins's later work on affect, is that these papers are not an outright rejection of the use of shock as a stimulus. They are neither simplistically antibehaviorist nor piously pro-psychoanalytic. Rather, these papers argue for a more complex interpretive approach to the experimental situation: how does a shock (or the threat of shock) activate different psychological needs and incite different responses from experimental subjects? Might an intensive engagement with a small number of subjects provide insight into the psychological power of a shock? Tomkins isn't so much picking sides in the intellectual battles between behaviorists and psychoanalysts and physiologists, between methods of experimentation and methods of association, as he is mixing together what each method might be able to contribute to an understanding of motivation and mind.

Most of Tomkins's work at the Harvard Psychological Clinic was devoted not to the elucidation of behaviorist paradigms but to the construction, validation, and use of projective techniques. Projective tests attempt to quantify the more open-ended free associations of a psychoanalytic or therapeutic encounter; they search for unconscious or unknown motivations that may not be available to be verbalized directly by a patient. These tests typically ask patients to talk about an ambiguous visual image (here the well-known Rorschach images are exemplary), and their responses are coded and scored to give a picture of the patient's cognitive, ideational, and emotional state: "an individual confronted with an ambiguous social situation and required to interpret it was likely to reveal his own personality in the process" (*Thematic Apperception Test,* 3). Murray and Christiana Morgan developed a projective test called the Thematic Apperception Test (TAT) at the clinic during the 1930s. It became a core component of the clinic's personological method and a widely used and well-validated test. The TAT is composed of a series of images depicting enigmatic situations: for example, in one card, a boy is looking at a violin lying on a table, his head in his hands (is he despondent? focused? bored? contemplative?). The patient is shown a series of picture cards like this and asked to create a dramatic story. With his wife, Elizabeth, Tomkins wrote an important scholarly guide to the TAT *(The Thematic Apperception Test: The Theory and Technique of Interpretation)* and began research that would lead to the standardization and publication of his own projective test in 1957 *(The Tomkins–Horn Picture Arrangement Test).*

While working at the clinic, Tomkins had not yet focused on the question of affect specifically, but he certainly began honing a technique for reading and remodeling disciplinary psychological knowledges and their relation to psychoanalysis that will underwrite his theory of affect in later decades. That work owes much to Murray's personological framework that invests in the intensive study of one individual by a variety of psychological methods: experimental, observational, projective, statistical, physiological, biographical, psychoanalytic. Mixing the genres of psychological research (the case history with measures of galvanic skin response, tests of hypnotic suggestibility, the telling of dramatic stories, and observations of the construction of dramatic scenes with toys, for example), Murray's personology strives for a kind of epistemological holism:

> The prevailing custom in psychology is to study one function or one aspect of an episode at a time—perception, emotion, intellection or behavior—and this is as it must be. The circumscription of attention is dictated by the need for detailed information. But the psychologist who does this should recognize that he is observing merely a part of an operating totality, and that this totality, in turn, is but a small temporal segment of a personality. (*Explorations in Personality*, 4)

We see three major ways in which Tomkins's affect theory is aligned with Murray's personology: their textual styles are akin, they have similar methodological ambitions, and they are both intensely engaged with Freudianism even as they cast doubt on some of Freud's central claims. Many of these likenesses can be tracked in Tomkins's contribution to a symposium, late in life for both men, on Murray's personological system. Indeed, much of what Tomkins writes in this short piece about Murray could, with little in the way of adjustment, be said of Tomkins himself: "the most salient feature of his thought is its conjoint scope and depth. It is not only a system; it is a very complex system that decomposes, grounds, and embeds the personality into overlapping systems of many dimensions" ("Personology Is a Complex, Lifelong, Never-Ending Enterprise," 608).

As Tomkins directly addresses Murray and his work, the differences between the men often fade, suggesting an ideo-affective intimacy between them. For example, as Tomkins quotes Murray's critique of Freud's theory of repetition compulsion, the cadence of Murray's writing seems to mirror Tomkins's own:

> This might be pretty nearly the whole truth *if* the genetical program, with its potentialities, ceased to operate at puberty; *if* the subject were not easily bored . . . *if* the human environment, parents, teachers, and peers were unanimous in their support of the same beliefs, codes, manners, political sentiments, and tastes; *if* the person were

not ambitious to emulate successively the more impressive performances and deeds of others, *if . . . if . . . if . . .* If it were not for these
and other self-realizing, novelty-seeking, ambitious, proudful,
imaginative, and creative dispositions in human beings, all of us
would stagnate with learned incapacities and a few enthralling
memories of infantile attachments. (610–11)

In this same piece we also see similarities between Tomkins and Murray
in their fondness for taxonomies that tend to drift away from any tightly
constrained structure. This is a tendency we have noticed not only in
Tomkins's published writing but also in his unpublished notes archived
at the Center for the History of Psychology—pages and pages and pages
of yellow legal notepaper taken up with classificatory lists and taxonomic rumination.

Tomkins remained in touch with Murray in the years after he left
Harvard for Princeton, CUNY, and Rutgers. Their written correspondence appears to be sparse, and Tomkins lays the blame for this on both
men. What is notable in the correspondence that has survived in archives
is the ways in which Tomkins mixes together Freudian and personological and affective claims in news about his professional and personal lives,
and (as with some of the published work) the lines between Tomkins
and Murray and Freud begin to blur. For example, there is a long letter in 1961 that recounts Tomkins's recent near-drowning experience.
This letter calls on Freudian notions of childhood experiences ("for the
first five years of my life my mother would not let me out of carriage"),
along with affective interpretations of the drowning event ("I was not
frightened, to my surprise as I think of it now, but ashamed"). Moreover,
despite Tomkins's career-long dedication to building a theory of affect
away from the confines of Cambridge, Massachusetts, he often seems
to be unable to draw a clear line between this work and Murray's, and
indeed between himself and Murray. In the final letter from Tomkins
held in Murray's papers, we see an ongoing ambivalence toward Murray
(drawing near out of love, yet at the same time offering sharp psychological interpretations of Murray that then turn into moments of self-
analysis and rumination about his own career). Contacting Murray in
the year before he (Murray) died, and seemingly in response to Murray's
final physical decline and a gift of some kind from him, Tomkins writes,

Dear Harry:

Your letter so saddened me. I loved your gift but I love you more—
do not leave us—verweile doch. From an excess of Satanic pride
our communication has been fitful and oblique, but the clock
keeps ticking. It tolls for you and for me. Your letter began my
mourning. It forced me to confront what the world and my world
will be when I cannot reach you. So I must reach you now. I cannot let you go without knowing that I understand your unholy
blend of Satan and Prometheus. Some years ago I asked you,
artlessly, what you would make of a Rembrandt who would not
exhibit his paintings. I pretended not to know, but I knew then
and I still know how guilt and shame shackle mortals who would
steal the sacred fire to illuminate the world. And how it feels to
have labored and struggled to give it shape and utterance, over
a lifetime, and to confront the possibility that time will run out
before the task is done, and done well enough. And how it feels to
confront the probability that even if it were done there might be
more to understand. There is no other psychologist of your scope
and depth and passion. I was reminded of that upon re-reading the
poem you wrote about me several years ago. Only recently have I
come to understand in myself what was so clear to you so long ago.
I have only, recently, in my 70th year been able, through self analysis, to defeat the albatross of my neurosis. Never really thought
it possible—but year by year the burden was lightened until one
night a few months ago I woke from a numinous dream immediately emancipated from a life long guilt I had carried all those years,
truly unconsciously. Before that was possible I had to confront terror, distress, rage and shame—all formidable—nonetheless masking
the deeper secret of guilt.

It is the lifting of that neurosis which prompts me to communicate
my deep love for your spirit and your nobility. It was that neurosis, as well as your own, which prohibited our friendship. I regret
that so much and the hour is late but not too late to tell you that I
understand you, appreciate your uniqueness and love you. I never
will forget you.

Silvan

FURTHER READING

Henry Murray has recounted the story about meeting Freud in a number of places. We draw our opening anecdote from James Anderson's interview with Murray ("An Interview with Henry A. Murray on His Meeting with Sigmund Freud"). Paul Roazen records the same story ("Interviews on Freud and Jung with Henry A. Murray in 1965"). Anderson's interview, Irving Alexander's biographical sketch of Tomkins, and Rodney Triplet's essay ("Harvard Psychology, the Psychological Clinic, and Henry A. Murray: A Case Study in the Establishment of Disciplinary Boundaries") have provided important historical background for our account of Tomkins's time at Harvard. It is worth noting that psychology, as an institutionalized field of inquiry at Harvard, began in 1876 when William James was appointed an assistant professor of psychology. However, for many decades, psychological research at Harvard was housed inside the Department of Philosophy. For a period, the department carried the name the Department of Philosophy and Psychology, making Tomkins's defection from philosophical research to psychological research less of an institutional leap than it might appear today. The disciplines of philosophy and psychology were formally separated at Harvard only in 1934, just prior to Tomkins's arrival in Cambridge. Triplet gives a detailed historical account of the intellectual, class, personal, and institutional politics at stake in the splitting of the department and the establishment of the Harvard Psychological Clinic.

Irving Alexander reports that Tomkins was in a seven-year analysis with Ruth Burr (a London-trained member of the Boston Psychoanalytic Society) for the treatment of "a severe reading block" ("Silvan S. Tomkins," 254). Our research into Ruth Burr has not uncovered any further information about his treatment with her. At a memorial for Tomkins at the American Psychological Association in August 1991, Brewster Smith (a colleague at Harvard) tells of living in a group house with Tomkins in 1941: "of the people in the house, five including Silvan were under psychoanalysis at the time" (video recording held in the Silvan S. Tomkins Papers at the Drs. Nicholas and Dorothy Cummings Center for the History of Psychology, University of Akron).

Tomkins's three early papers on the phenomenology of electric shock are "An Analysis of the Use of Electric Shock with Human Subjects," "Experimental Study of Anxiety," and "An Apparatus for the Study of Motor Learning under Threat of Electric Shock" (this last copublished with Henry Gerbrands). The two letters from Tomkins to Murray described here can be found in the Henry A. Murray Papers at the Harvard University Archives (HUGFP 97.6, box 22, Murray, Henry A., Correspondence: General— T-U 1910–1986, Folder: 1960–1987 T). In 1963, Murray wrote poems for each of the contributors to *The Study of Lives: Essays on Personality in Honor of Henry A. Murray* (White, 1963) which had been presented to him on the occasion of his seventieth birthday. His poem for Tomkins, titled "Graves (S. T.)," is contained in a volume titled *Leaves of Green Memories* that is held at the Drs. Nicholas and Dorothy Cummings Center for the History of Psychology, University of Akron.

12
CYBERNETICS

What was it about *cybernetics,* that remarkably cross-disciplinary body of research of the 1940s and 1950s, that so appealed to Silvan Tomkins? Not just Tomkins, of course. Cybernetics fascinated many thinkers in the years immediately following World War II and in the longer postwar moment: mathematicians, engineers, neurophysiologists, anthropologists, sociologists, psychiatrists, philosophers, writers, artists, and musicians of the psychedelic/cybernetic 1960s. A recent upswing in history and criticism has begun to unearth the relevance of cybernetics (and its close cousin, information theory) for the postwar moment, especially for those thinkers associated with canonical French theory (Derrida, Foucault, Lacan, Levi-Strauss, and others) as it has come to be known and taught in the North American academy. From the perspective of these histories, mid-century structuralism appears to have been so thoroughly imbued with cybernetics and information theory that one writer has suggested that "a great deal of what we now call French theory was already a translation of American theory" (Liu, 291) while another has proposed the term "cybernetic structuralism" (Geoghegan, 111). Tomkins contributed to this transatlantic conversation. As we noted in chapter 1, he presented his understanding of the affect system at the Fourteenth International Congress of Psychology in a paper that was published in French in a collection edited by Jacques Lacan. "Le modele que nous présenterions," wrote Tomkins's translator, "serait un systeme d'intercommunication qui recoit, transmet, traduit et transforme les messages conscients et inconscients. Quel sont les interlocuteurs et de quoi parlent-ils? Voila la question." (We present a model of a communications system that receives, transmits, translates, and transforms conscious and unconscious messages. Who or what is communicating and what is being talked about? That is the question.) In Tomkins's model, the human being becomes a loose, complex assemblage, structured and motivated by information flows and feedback between numerous mechanisms. Lacan must have appreciated how, in this model, the circulation of messages (the letter) becomes the reality of the psyche.

In this section, we draw on our previous discussions of Tomkins's use of cybernetic ideas (chapters 4 and 7) to unfold his concept of the central assembly. At the same time, we are curious about the broader, somewhat contradictory epistemic and political fates of cybernetics. On one hand, cybernetics appears to be a universalizing, imperializing "Manichean science" (Galison, 232) that evolved directly out of the context of war and is still imprinted with this context. On the other hand, cybernetics is "a form of life" (Pickering, 9), radically open ended and forward looking, characterized by protean application rather than utterly determined by its military origins. By the mid-1960s (that is, just after the publication of the first two volumes of *AIC*), as enthusiasm ebbed and funding structures disappeared, cybernetics as such became marginalized in the natural and social sciences, while its most significant ideas were integrated into or dispersed among other fields. No doubt, the ongoing difficulty of integrating Tomkins's work into the theoretical humanities has something to do with his belated commitment to terminology and ideas that came to have a highly ambivalent political and epistemological status. Cybernetics continues to hover in the background of so much discourse on the posthuman, a crucial, formative element in the genealogy of our present moment whose role is just beginning to be understood.

Tomkins was no orthodox cybernetician, if such a thing ever existed. From the mid-1930s to the late 1940s, he worked at the Harvard Psychological Clinic (see chapter 11), just up the avenue from Norbert Wiener at MIT, whose book *Cybernetics; or, Control and Communication in the Animal and the Machine* (1948) defined the field and its many applications. Neither mathematician (like Wiener and John von Neumann), engineer (like Julian Bigelow), nor neurophysiologist (like Arturo Rosenblueth and Warren McCulloch), Tomkins would have fit more comfortably with the second cluster of participants at the Macy Conferences on Cybernetics (1946–53), those psychologists and social scientists (including Gregory Bateson, Margaret Mead, and others) interested in the value of cybernetic ideas for the human sciences. These ideas included a redescription of goal-directed or purposive behavior in engineering terms and a commitment to a model of circular causality, in particular, the central role of negative feedback in self-correction. Seemingly applicable across enormous domains, these cybernetic ideas raised hopes that a formal, computational approach to complex, reflexive aspects of human phenomena and behavior could be developed. No less functionalist than structuralist, cybernetics engaged the psychologists, psychiatrists, and psychoanalysts who participated in the Macy Conferences by bringing together various psychological approaches to mind and brain: discarding any unified notion of will or intention, cyberneticians spoke the language of behaviorism, yet, at the same time, emphasized unconscious purposes or goals. As Evelyn Fox Keller puts it, cybernetics "aimed at the mechanical implementation of exactly the kind of purposive organization of which Kant had written and that was so vividly exemplified by biological organisms; in other words, a science that would repudiate the very distinction between organism and machine on which the concept of *self-organization* was originally predicated" (65). Such a non-Kantian, broadly monist approach that spanned the human and natural sciences certainly appealed to Tomkins, whose commitment to nondualist thinking and disposition toward organized complexity (a term coined by Warren Weaver) led him to integrate cybernetic ideas into his theoretical apparatus.

First, and perhaps most significantly, cybernetics assisted Tomkins in conceptualizing the human being as a loose assemblage of interrelated systems. "From the outset," wrote Tomkins not long after retiring from his university teaching, "I have supposed the person to be a bio-psycho-social entity at the intersect of both more complex higher social systems and lower biological systems" ("Quest," 308). These distinct systems (biological, psychological, sociological) are not reducible to one another but rather exist in relations of dependence on, as well as independence from, one another. Tomkins insists on a looseness of fit between and within systems, at all scales, especially the biological. His uses of evolutionary theory (see chapter 3 and the interlude on Darwin) undergird this understanding:

> The critical point is that **the human being has evolved as a multi-mechanism system in which each mechanism is at once incomplete but essential to the functioning of the system as a whole.**

The affect mechanism is distinct from the sensory, motor, memory, cognitive, pain, and drive mechanisms as all of these are distinct from the heart, circulatory, respiratory, liver, kidney, and other parts of the general homeostatic system. (319–20)

Note that the human as "multimechanism system" is by no means the perfected creature that we hear about in so many encomiums to the design skills of natural selection. It is something distinctly more hodge-podge, a result of "multiple criteria" for adaptation that result in what Tomkins calls "play," that is, "a very loose fit in the match between one mechanism and every other mechanism, between the system as a whole and its various environments, and reproductive success" (320). While play within and between systems is crucial, it is nevertheless limited by criteria of survival and reproduction: "although the principle of 'play' cautions against the possibility of an ideal fit, the second principle argues for sufficient limitation of mismatch to meet a satisficing criterion, that the system as a whole is good enough to reproduce itself" (320).

The "good enough" assemblage may be one of Tomkins's most durable ideas. It characterizes not only the human assemblage as a whole but various mechanisms or subsystems as well. Affect, in particular, "is a loosely matched mechanism evolved to play a number of parts in continually changing assemblies of mechanisms" (320). In this context, Tomkins offers, once again, a familiar structuralist metaphor: "It [affect] is in some respects like a letter of an alphabet in a language, changing in significance as it is assembled with varying other letters to form different words, sentences, paragraphs. Further, the system has no single 'output.' 'Behavior' is of neither more nor less importance than feeling" (320–21). While it has been common to represent the turn to affect in the 1990s as a response to an exclusive emphasis in the theoretical humanities on linguistic signification, it strikes us that any too-rigid opposition between affect, on one hand, and code, language, or signifying system, on the other, has not yet fully taken into account the cybernetic context for structuralism.

By his own account, Tomkins's conception of the assemblage took shape via the "fantasy of a machine, fearfully and wonderfully made in the image of man . . . no less human than automated" (308–9), which prompted an extended thought experiment (see our brief discussion in chapter 4). Wiener's writings offered Tomkins "the concept of multiple assemblies of varying degrees of independence, dependence, interdependence, and control and transformation of one by another" (309), which led to his understanding of affect as an amplifying "co-assembly" (309).

Again, the image of the human that one gets reading Tomkins is not the streamlined, tightly organized, perfected cyborg but rather "an integrated automaton—with microscopic and telescopic lenses and sonar ears, with atomic powered arms and legs, with a complex feedback circuitry powered by a generalizing intelligence obeying equally general motives having the characteristics of human affects" (1:119). This monstrous "generalizing intelligence" differs from the chess-playing artificial intelligence that would come into the historical foreground just as cybernetics faded into the background. Tomkins turned to the computer as a tool to model personality, not intelligence. In his contribution to the edited volume *Computer Simulation of Personality* (1963), Tomkins assesses various attitudes toward the computer in seeking a middle ground between those who "love and worship only a machine, because they are alienated from themselves as they are from others" and those who reject the machine, a rejection "based on alienation of the individual from that part of nature which is impersonal" ("Computer Simulation," 5). Two decades before computers entered the home, Tomkins sought "to be at home with the computer" (7), "neither [to] derogate nor idealize himself or the computer" (7), and recognized the enormous possibilities of automated computation as well as its limits. The computer, he suggests, is "a complexity amplifier" (7) that is conceptually neutral; that encourages creative, constructive thought; and that (perhaps most significantly) "places a premium on clarity. **The computer is sufficiently concrete minded, sufficiently moronic, so that the theorist must be meticulous, certain and detailed in how he instructs the computer, whose favorite response seems to be 'huh?'"** (8). Computer simulation, Tomkins argues, is less an instrumental criterion (of intelligence, say) than it is expressive of theory or a vehicle for ideas.

Although Tomkins's research program did not directly involve the new computers (as far as we know), it did rely on the powerful idea of automated computation and the accompanying cybernetic understanding of communication as control in the human animal. In the last volume of *AIC*, subtitled *Cognition: Duplication and Transformation of*

Information, Tomkins unfolds what he calls "the second half of human being theory" (4:1), the cognitive system in complex interaction with the motivational mechanisms, the affects and drives (see chapter 14). In a brief preface, Tomkins explains that he wrote most of this volume in 1955 but was distracted by the birth of his child and surprised by "the unexpected riches of affect" (xv), which became the focus of the first two volumes of *AIC.* He warns, "The contemporary reader may find the bulk of it both new and unfamiliar and old and dated. It was written 40 years ago, and I found little reason to change it. In some quarters it will be as persuasive or unpersuasive as it would have been in 1955" (xv). This last (or is it first?) volume of *AIC* did little to assist Tomkins's reputation when it was published in the early 1990s. We are curious about its possible reception now, when ever more embedded digital technologies and exponentially increasing automation capacities are bringing questions of minded machines into the foreground. It's not difficult to imagine the fictional designers in the HBO television show *Westworld,* say, consulting *AIC* as they script personalities for their life-like, conscious androids.

Consciousness, of course, is the third major term in the title of *AIC.* Tomkins tackles the topic directly in a chapter on "The Central Assembly: The Limited Channel of Consciousness," which begins with an evolutionary understanding of consciousness as connected with motility: "We find consciousness in animals who move about in space but not in organisms rooted in the earth" (4:288). The problem, as Tomkins puts it in information theoretical terms, is

the magnitude of new information necessary from moment to moment as the world changed, as the organism moved. The solution to this problem consisted in receptors that were capable of registering the constantly changing state of the environment, transmission lines that carried this information to a central site for analysis, and above all, **a transformation of these messages into conscious form so that the animal "knew" what was going on and could govern his behavior by this information.** (4:289)

Tomkins defines consciousness in terms of a particular kind of information duplication that he calls *transmutation,* "a unique type of duplication by which some aspects of the world reveal themselves to another part of the same world" (4:290). Interestingly, Tomkins conceives of this process, by which an unconscious message is transformed into a conscious report, as "biophysical or biochemical in nature and that it will eventually be possible to synthesize this process" (4:290)—consciousness as a biological phenomenon that can, in principle, be fabricated. "Fabricating consciousness is, of course, a very different matter from constructing 'thinking' machines. These, we assume, are intelligent but nonconscious" (4:290): Tomkins bypasses the tradition in AI and philosophy of mind that conceives of intelligence solely in relation to complex symbol manipulation in favor of a biological theory of consciousness.

In his (quite technical) review of the neurophysiological literature of the 1950s on central inhibition of sensory information, Tomkins pays particular attention to the cognitive psychologist George A. Miller's famous paper "The Magic Number Seven, Plus or Minus Two: Some Limits on Our Capacity for Processing Information" (1956). As engaged as he is by the empirical data, he is not persuaded by the idea of an inherent channel capacity in human information processing. Instead, Tomkins proposes what he calls the "central assembly," a collection of conscious reports that are functionally related to a central matching mechanism (see our discussion of imagery in chapter 7). What is admitted to the central assembly is "a compromise between centrally retrieved information and sensory input [in which] the relative contribution of sensory and central information is presumed to vary" (4:306). That is, rather than any inherent channel capacity (we are only ever consciously aware of approximately seven discrete objects), Tomkins proposes a highly changeable awareness dependent on competing, multiple variables: **"As this assembly is disassembled and reassembled from competing sources, then conscious reports continually change from moment to moment"** (4:306). Consciousness, for Tomkins, is a "semistable psychological structure" (4:306) that is constantly being (dis)assembled through a process of central matching. The individual's awareness is of "centrally emitted imagery" that matches either sensory or memory input or, most commonly, some combination of the two. The changeability of the central assembly is crucial: there is no single channel, no unchanging self that is conscious or that an individual is always conscious of. Instead, the key question becomes, **"What are the principles** by which a person seeks or avoids information or selects or excludes it?" (4:307). This question of selective attention becomes a special case of motivated behavior.

We can see how intertwined Tomkins's cybernetic, information-processing account of consciousness is with his affect theory. We can also see the importance of Freud, once again, who, as Tomkins puts it, "revolutionized the theory of awareness by explaining the process as a derivative [of] motivation" (4:312). While he disagreed with the Freudian premise that unconscious wishes underlie all behavior, or even, for that matter, all dreams (many of which he considered to be confrontations with unsolved problems or unfinished business [4:310]), Tomkins nonetheless insisted that "a general theory must bring back to the problem of consciousness the nonmotivational factors that the revolution minimized but without surrendering the gains won by Freud" (4:313). In the 1950s, it was the cyberneticians (the "neurophysiologists and automata designers" [4:313]) who had the potential to bring psychoanalytic and behaviorist-cognitive insights together ("cybernetic bedfellows," as he calls them [*Perspectives in Personality,* 153]). This alliance made sense of the role of consciousness, in Freud's understanding, as "a sensory organ for perceiving psychic qualities" (*Interpretation,* 407) and, in Tomkins's cybernetic understanding, as it emerges from the transmutation of selected information. Perhaps the ongoing promise of cybernetic theory, which was also the promise of structuralism in some of its incarnations, lies in how it suspends the opposition between biological, psychological, and sociological explanations for what is (and is not) selected to become conscious. Of course, in suspending these oppositions, cybernetics also risks the imperializing tendencies of a science-of-everything that translates philosophical issues into engineering or design problems. These risks are only more relevant today than they were sixty years ago.

FURTHER READING

Tomkins discusses the significance of Wiener's writing on cybernetics for his initial development of affect theory in "The Quest for Primary Motives: Biography and Autobiography of an Idea." Only an abstract of the conference paper in which he presents an early formulation of these ideas, "Consciousness and the Unconscious in a Model of the Human Being," has been preserved in *Proceedings of the 14th International Congress of Psychology*. The paper itself, translated by Muriel Cahen, appeared as "La conscience et l'inconscient representes dans un modele de l'être humain" in *La Psychanalyse* (1956), edited by Lacan. This material was revised for inclusion in various chapters of *AIC1*. Tomkins's interest in computation appears across all the volumes of *AIC* but most explicitly in two chapters of *AIC4*, "The Central Assembly: The Limited Channel of Consciousness" (chapter 13) and "The Feedback Mechanism: Consciousness, the Image, and the Motoric" (chapter 14). For more on the computers of the 1960s, see his introduction to *Computer Simulation of Personality* (1963), a volume he coedited with Samuel Messick; see also his commentary on essays by Gerald Blum and A. R. Luria that appear in *Perspectives in Personality Research* (1960), edited by Henry P. David and J. C. Brengelmann.

The scholarly literature on cybernetics has been accumulating in recent years. On French translations of "American theory," see Lydia Liu's "The Cybernetic Unconscious: Rethinking Lacan, Poe, and French Theory." On cybernetic structuralism, see Bernard Dionysius Geoghegan's helpful genealogy "From Information Theory to French Theory: Jakobson, Lévi-Strauss, and the Cybernetic Apparatus." On the military origins of cybernetics in Wiener's work on antiaircraft guidance systems and the goal of predicting the behavior of an intelligent adversary, see Peter Galison's "The Ontology of the Enemy: Norbert Wiener and the Cybernetic Vision." And on cybernetics as an open-ended "form of life" and its many political and aesthetic manifestations, see Andrew Pickering's *The Cybernetic Brain: Sketches of Another Future*. For a detailed history of the Macy Conferences and their participants, see Steve Joshua Heims's *The Cybernetics Group*. We consulted several other works, including Céline Lafontaine's "The Cybernetic Matrix of 'French Theory,'" Evelyn Fox Keller's "Organisms, Machines, and Thunderstorms: A History of Self-Organization, Part One" and "Part Two," Heather A. Love's "Cybernetic Modernism and the Feedback Loop: Ezra Pound's Poetics of Transmission," and Christopher Johnson's "'French' Cybernetics."

For an analysis of the role of affect and intersubjectivity in early artificial intelligence, see Elizabeth A. Wilson's *Affect and Artificial Intelligence*. It strikes us that Tomkins's biological theory of consciousness shares some intellectual filiation with Gerald Edelman's, especially in its emphasis on neural reentry. See *The Remembered Present* and *Bright Air, Brilliant Fire*.

13
THE PSYCHOLOGY
OF KNOWLEDGE

It is tempting to those of us trained in structuralist and poststructuralist thinking of the last forty years to dismiss Tomkins's case study of Karl Marx (3:309–20) as an unfortunate instance of psychologizing explanation. How dispiriting is it to encounter an argument that the roots of Marx's astonishing critique of capitalism can be found in his relationship with his father and, what evolved from this, a redemptive, reparative script that played out in many other aspects of his life, including his relationship with Engels? Yet to dismiss Tomkins's analysis would be to ignore an acute description of a powerful affective organization, one that has been enormously influential or (in terms that Marx might have used) world-historical. According to Tomkins, the polarizing script that Marx invented involves "a magnification, a purification and idealization, of both heaven and hell and of the heroic strategy necessary to defeat Satan and regain paradise" (3:309); it is a script "committed to instrumental activity, but at the same time utterly intolerant of any suggestion of meliorism" (3:309). Marx's "creative genius" (3:309) lay precisely in how the script he developed offered new solutions to problems that were at once personal and, in some sense, shared:

> Although some creative artists and scientists literally project the structure of their own past history into their creations, it is much more common that the creator achieves a *solution* which is *new* rather than a simple restatement of his personal struggle with his own destiny. . . . **To the extent to which there are commonalities between his own problems and those of humanity at large, his new solution may be more or less relevant to the general human condition.** (3:311)

Rather than offering a reductive psychological explanation, then, Tomkins seeks to explore a fundamental question: how does new knowledge emerge from personal experience?

The insight that biography has some bearing on styles of thinking and object choice, that (say) Marx's contributions to political economy are personally motivated, should be uncontroversial. But it is not easy to specify the role of biographical experience in accounts of knowledge without sounding dismissive of the knowledge itself. This has something to do with the disciplinary (and extradisciplinary) status of psychology, those shifting relations of authority between psychology and philosophy indexed by the term *psychologism*. As Dale Jacquette explains in his genealogy of the concept, this most deprecatory of attributions has its origins in late nineteenth-century philosophy:

> The objections, if not the vehemence with which antipsychologists frequently raise objections against psychologism, can generally be attributed to the assumption that an empirical psychology of subjective thought cannot be expected to explain logically necessary objective truths, especially those of logic, semantics, and mathematics, but also of any field in which a sharp distinction is supposed to hold between objective truths and subjective perceptions of the truth. ("Psychologism," 313)

Psychologism can now be imputed to any explanation of a literary, cultural, or sociopolitical phenomenon that makes psychology primary. Anyone who has taught a literature class and encountered a student's bland, condescending diagnosis of an author ("was s/he depressed when s/he wrote that?") knows the perils of psychologism, as does anyone who encounters facile attributions of individual motives in popular, mass, or social media that purport to explain complex dynamics of class, race, gender, or sexuality while disavowing institutional histories and the structural consequences of power. But is it possible not to throw the baby of the psyche out with the bathwater of psychologism? What role, if any, might psychology play in accounts of knowledge today?

These questions, which challenge contemporary thinking in the theoretical humanities, are implicitly posed by Tomkins's many case studies of writers, performers, and other public figures littered throughout volumes 2 and 3 of *AIC*. There is something fascinatingly gossipy about these studies, replete with letters, journal entries, and biographical bits, which range in length from brief notes (on Ernest Hemingway, say, or Oliver North) to more substantial analyses (of Tolstoy, Eugene O'Neill, and others) to nearly full-blown psychobiographies of some major figures (Chekhov, Freud, Marx). These case studies exemplify, illustrate, and give body to Tomkins's theoretical approach to development, script theory, and personality (see our discussions in chapters 8 and 9). For example, we may read sections titled "Monopolistic Shame, Contempt, Self-Contempt, Anger and Fear: The Sullen, Defiant Mouse of Dostoevsky" (2:483–96), "Ludwig Wittgenstein: Nuclear Decontamination Script for Sexuality, Disgust, and Anger" (3:359–65), or (one of our favorites) "The Depressive Posture in the Comic Performer" (3:326–31) on Judy Garland and Jackie Gleason.

At the same time, these case studies offer forays into a hypothetical field that Tomkins defined in his 1965 essay "Affect and the Psychology of Knowledge":

> Such a field would concern itself first of all with the structure of man's knowledge. This would include both knowledge which is demonstrably valid and knowledge which is demonstrably invalid, and knowledge which is gray and especially knowledge which is based on faith. It would also concern itself with the ebb and flow of affect investment in ideas and ideology, in method and styles of investigation, and in what is considered acceptable criteria of evidence. (73)

This was Tomkins's bid to bring affect theory into dialogue with the history and philosophy of science as well as the sociology of knowledge. As the term *structure* would imply—Thomas Kuhn's *The Structure of Scientific Revolutions* had appeared just three years earlier—Tomkins hoped that affect theory could offer resources to emerging critical and historical studies of scientific knowledge. This hope was not unfounded: in the mid-1960s, Kuhn described his own contribution in terms of psychology and, in the 1970s, turned to gestalt psychology to rethink aspects of the incommensurability of paradigms. By contrast, the most prominent or popular uptakes of Kuhn's ideas were sociological ones, especially those that assimilated the concept of paradigm (in the particular sense of worldview, one of the many senses that Kuhn would distance himself from) with Foucault's notion of episteme. The macro-scale at which these ideas applied appeared to foreclose the relevance of individual psychology.

For Tomkins, however, the "structure" of knowledge refers not only to institutional practices, histories, and techniques (such as the separation of the disciplines or the problem sets at the end of chemistry textbook chapters) but also to the ways that a biologically differentiated affect system, in conjunction with a specific individual's developmental trajectory, sets up epistemological motives. As always, Tomkins urges the integration of biological, psychological, sociological, and literary or cultural methods in a "complete science of man" (72), but this is not a call for consilience, that is, an integration of knowledge under the rubric of one existing method or science (see our discussion of consilience at the end of chapter 3). Rather, it is distinctly multidisciplinary: "We do *not* intend by this . . . to argue for the superiority of one method over the other. Invariances found in the library through an examination of beliefs which men have held over centuries are not necessarily any less lawful than those found in the laboratory" (72–73). The archaeological method that Foucault practiced and theorized—and his own rigorous antipsychologism—need not stand in complete opposition to Tomkins's psychological enterprise, itself no less literary and historical than experimental and clinical.

No less political, either. The term around which Tomkins centers his discussion of the psychology of knowledge is neither paradigm nor episteme but ideology (see chapter 10). Ideology is more specific than worldview. Distinguishing it from both fact and fiction, Tomkins associates ideology fundamentally with controversy: "At the growing edge of the frontier of all sciences there necessarily is a maximum of uncertainty, and what is lacking in evidence is filled by passion and faith, and hatred and scorn for the disbelievers. *Science will never be free of ideology, though yesterday's ideology is today's fact or fiction*" (73). Tomkins implies that the imbrication of facts with values is a consequence of the relations between ideas and affects. He analyzes these relations by way of the following terms: ideo-affective posture, defined as "any *loosely organized* set of feelings and *ideas about feelings*" (74); ideology, defined as "any *highly organized* and articulate set of *ideas about anything*" (74); and ideo-affective resonance. A given ideology (which, for Tomkins, appears to be a specific type of script) resonates more or less well with the feelings and ideas that it attempts to organize. Tomkins likens the relation between ideo-affective posture and ideology to a love affair in which "the fit need not at the outset be perfect" (74). Reciprocity over time may lead to a better match between feelings and organized ideas, or it may not. Indeed, ideo-affective resonance is highly contingent and historically variable. For example, "a politically conservative ideology in a democratic society might be much less conservative than the ideo-affective resonance would have made attractive had the individual lived in a feudal society" (75). (A contemporary example: the loosely organized ideo-affective postures of Trump and his supporters might better fit the ideologies of an explicitly authoritarian society.)

Tomkins's analysis sometimes sounds like Louis Althusser's analysis of the role of ideology in reproducing the relations of production. Tomkins writes, "The ideology is a part of the social whole which not only expresses the feelings and ideas of its present members but helps to create in the next generation the same kind of socialized human beings through influencing the socialization and social structure to either maintain or to better approximate the general ideology" (76). But Tomkins emphasizes the dynamic, historically shifting, and reciprocal resonances between ideologies and those affective experiences they organize and express. (Perhaps, in this respect, Raymond Williams's notions of dominant, residual, and emergent are more compatible.) Writing in the 1960s and acutely aware of decolonization movements and global political transformation, Tomkins suggests that Marxist ideology (but also American ideology, more on which in a moment) can become "acceptable to a society which has ideas and feelings which no longer resonate to traditional ideologies" (77). Tomkins stresses the dangers of a poor fit between such ideologies and a given society's actual ideo-affective postures: "the modernization of a society under the directive of a poorly fitting ideology may subject the members of that society as well as other societies to excessive strain in the attempt to accommodate to the somewhat alien ideology" (77). Owing to centralized media control, however, in a generation or two, such strains may recede: "in modern times the concentration of power and the means of communication in the hands of an elite enables the control of society through the dissemination of the revolutionary ideology" (77).

While Tomkins's writing on ideology may, in places, sound like Marxist-materialist thinking (and may well be available for such use), he is not a fellow traveler. Rather, he suggests that Marxism has become the major world ideology of the 1960s because "the ideology which powered the American and French Revolutions has yet to be modernized" (77). Such modernization is a task for the new field, the psychology of knowledge, and he alerts his readers to the urgency of this Cold War task. He begins with a sense of the resonances between loosely organized ideo-affective postures in the United States and Western Europe (freedom, the rights of the individual, freedom of speech) with an "as yet unformulated ideology for modern times for a highly industrialized society" (78) before proposing

> a commitment of major energies, under forced draft [!], to the world-wide study of man in a war of man against those aspects of man which restrict his freedom and development. A sense of urgency about the possible benefits of self-knowledge achieved through the scientific study of man is needed as much and as urgently as the atomic bomb was needed in the second World War. These benefits include the control of war and discrimination . . . the radical enrichment of experience . . . a renewal of the awareness of the significance of the individual as an innovator on the extended frontier which reaches from the virgin land to the endless frontiers of art and science . . . a renewal of the awareness of one's identification with all human beings in a common effort to solve our collective human problems . . . the sense of solidarity and pride of being a member of the human race. (78)

Here Tomkins unveils a modernized Enlightenment liberalism or Kantian cosmopolitanism with an Emersonian twist. In the postwar logic, a universalizing American Transcendentalism has the potential to offer a synthesis of what he defines, in his polarity scale, as left and right ideologies (again, see chapter 10). As he puts it later in the essay, **"the middle of the road represents the most radical ideology rather** than a compromise . . . a creative synthesis evokes some resonance from both sides" (86). For Tomkins, exemplary representatives of such synthetic positions include Kant, Beethoven, and Whitehead, and we might wish to include Kuhn as well.

Tomkins would consider his own cross-disciplinary cybernetic commitments to biology, psychology, sociology, and literature as another attempt at such a creative synthesis. It is difficult to know how to read these pages and their aggressive epistemological-political program in a current context that has inherited cognate global programs but entirely set aside what, for Tomkins, would provide their justification and basis: a theory of affect and value. What genealogies might be drawn between contemporary world-ecological conceptions and this earlier moment of global consciousness if they were to take Tomkins into account? Consider his essay contribution to a volume titled *Interdisciplinary Relationships in the Social Sciences* (1969) in which Tomkins compares biological, psychological, and social systems and offers a prescient understanding of how information growth creates social and political dilemmas: "complex systems . . . suffer three critical vulnerabilities which are inherent to their growth" ("Personality Theory and Social Science," 201), what he calls *mismatch and discoordination, increasing rigidities,* and *overstress.* Under such circumstances, "that society will continue to *grow* which most nurtures its mutations, its dissident minorities who provide it with new viable alternatives" (202); he turns to international communities, especially of science, as a model for other political institutions. What are the similarities and differences between Tomkins's vision and that of, say, Bruno Latour's project *An Inquiry into Modes of Existence*?

To pose a more general question about the psychology of knowledge: how would an approach such as Tomkins's that foregrounds the relations between subjectivity and knowledge inflect a science studies that has for the most part bracketed subjectivity except insofar as it relates to questions of objectivity? Tomkins offers a distinct set of tools for thinking reflexively about the *subjectivity–knowledge* continuum. In a 1976 essay "On the Subjectivity of Personality Theory," Tomkins, with his cowriter George A. Atwood, explores the inevitable links between theory making and subjectivity. The writers analyze the work of three personality theorists in the context of biography and autobiography with this goal: "**By clarifying the ways in which theoretical ideas are conditioned by the personality of the theorist, this interpretive process transforms the subjectivity inhering in present systems into an explicit object of investigation**" (170). Atwood and Tomkins insist that "the psychological analysis of a personality theory is not an attempt to explain away its concepts; its purpose is rather to assess and understand the theorist's underlying vision of the human situation" (170), and to assert that their approach "represents only one branch of a larger discipline which would study the role of subjective factors in the structure of man's knowledge in general" (177). In the field that Tomkins called the psychology of knowledge, theory can and should "turn back on itself" (167), that is, it should situate itself in both psychological and sociological terms. These perspectives, for Tomkins, are never opposed to one another, although they may be limited, in his discourse, by the category of "the human situation." We wonder how a differently situated approach that nevertheless takes the subjectivity of both theory and theorist seriously could be brought into genealogical and conceptual relation to science studies today.

FURTHER READING

Our discussion here is largely based on "Affect and the Psychology of Knowledge," an essay that appeared in the volume *Affect, Cognition, and Personality: Empirical Studies* (1965) that Tomkins coedited with Carroll Izard. Tomkins revised his discussion of ideology in this essay for inclusion in the chapter on "Ideology and Anger" (chapter 8) of *AIC3*. We also consulted "Personality Theory and Social Science" (1969), Tomkins and George A. Atwood's "On the Subjectivity of Personality Theory" (1976), and Tomkins's homage to Henry Murray, "Personology Is a Complex, Lifelong, Never-Ending Enterprise" (1987). We encourage interested readers to look at the case studies of authors and thinkers in *AIC2* and *AIC3*.

On the question of psychologism, please see Dale Jacquette's "Psychologism the Philosophical Shibboleth" and his edited volume *Philosophy, Psychology, and Psychologism* (2003). It is of interest that Kuhn titled his response to Karl Popper, presented at the 1965 International Symposium on the Philosophy of Science, "Logic of Discovery or Psychology of Research?" with the latter naming his own approach. For an excellent discussion of Kuhn's relation to psychoanalysis and psychology, see John Forrester's "On Kuhn's Case: Psychoanalysis and the Paradigm" in *Thinking in Cases*. In more recent science studies, subjectivity has been approached by way of a Foucauldian framework as what must be shaped or disciplined so that distinct varieties of objectivity can emerge (see Lorraine Daston and Peter Galison, *Objectivity*). While we have found no direct evidence that Tomkins read Foucault, we did find both a heavily marked-up clipping of Ian Hacking's long review of Foucault's work in the *New York Review of Books* from May 14, 1981, and a page of notes titled "Magnification + Foucault" in Tomkins's papers at the Archives of the History of American Psychology, Drs. Nicholas and Dorothy Cummings Center for the History of Psychology, University of Akron (Depot Box 5-1 Folder A).

14
THE MINDING SYSTEM

At the beginning of the fourth and final volume of *AIC,* Tomkins surprises his reader. He announces that the prior three volumes have been but one-half of what he calls his "human being theory" (4:1). Having described drives, affects, scripts, various subcortical systems, and their interdependencies in these first three volumes, Tomkins turns to a topic that seems to have been on his mind from the first: *cognition.* He proposes that an examination of the cognitive system alongside his prior work on affects, drives, and neurology will be the basis for a general theory of personality. The work on affect and scripts, it seems, has been a "prolegomenon" (1) to this more expansive account of human psychology.

This announcement arrives as a surprise not simply because Tomkins appears to be turning from one topic (affect) to another (cognition) but because he is asking his reader to attend to a psychological process that, in the earlier volumes, he claimed has been consistently overvalued in psychological theory. Indeed, much of the rhetorical purchase of the first three volumes of *AIC* comes from Tomkins's sustained and pointed critique of the dominance of cognition in psychological research. Volume 3, in particular, makes a strong argument that cognitive theory has become "imperialistic" (3:38)—in the wake of the so-called cognitive revolution of the 1960s and 1970s, psychology had become too focused on cognitive mechanisms. With cognitive theory in the ascendency (and behaviorism and psychoanalysis in retreat), many researchers came to see mind as coterminous with cognition, and the concurrent rise of new digital technologies (e.g., the increasing power of integrated circuits and the development of silicon chips) encouraged an identification of cognition and mind with a reductive mode of computation: "complex inner processes could be simplified and objectified" (4:4). Eventually, Tomkins argues, psychological researchers came to devalue the motivational nature of emotion, they operationalized cognition as a process that functions independently of affects and drives, and they placed cognition in an executive position—standing over and managing these other, ancillary psychological events.

Tomkins's criticism of Stanley Schachter and Jerome Singer's widely influential experiment about emotional states can be taken as exemplary of his concerns about the imperialism of cognitive theory in psychology. In 1962, Schachter and Singer argued that emotion could best be understood as a function of the cognitive appraisal of a physiological state:

> An emotional state may be considered a function of a state of physiological arousal and of a cognition appropriate to this state of arousal. The cognition, in a sense, exerts a steering function. Cognitions arising from the immediate situation as interpreted by past experience provide the framework within which one understands and labels his feelings. It is the cognition which determines whether the state of physiological arousal will be labeled as "anger," "joy," "fear," or whatever. (380)

They conclude that "cognitive factors are potent determiners of emotional states" (398). Tomkins was unpersuaded—epistemologically and phenomenologically. For him, emotion was more than simply the labeling of a physiological state:

> Surely no one who has experienced joy at one time and rage at another time would suppose that these radically different feelings were really the same, except for different "interpretations" placed upon similar "arousals." **Only a science which had come to radically discount conscious experience would have taken such an explanation seriously.** (3:44–45)

Tomkins contends that the cognitive theories that colonized psychology tend too much toward simplicity of explanation and are inclined to make sharp distinctions between the various subsystems of mind at the expense of reading for inter- and intrasystem affiliations: **"our present generation of cognizers do not love affect less, but they do love cognition more and love it not wisely but too well"** (3:48). That is, these cognitively oriented researchers came to position cognition in opposition to drives, they subsumed affect under mechanisms of appraisal, and they undertheorized the ways in which affects and drives and cognitions conjoin and disjoin.

In the light of these assessments, Tomkins's turn toward cognition in *AIC4* is likely to feel like something of a surprise. In the first volume of *AIC,* Tomkins describes the affect of surprise as a "general interrupter to ongoing activity . . . a circuit breaker" (1:498–99; see also chapter 5). That is, surprise will have the effect, like a special announcement (breaking news!) on the radio or TV, of interrupting the current program and orienting the individual's attention away from one thing to another. If Tomkins's turn to cognition in the final volume of *AIC* is a surprise, and if it orients our focus, for the moment, away from affects and drives and scripts, to what is Tomkins trying to draw our attention? What would he like us to consider now that we have been oriented in this new direction?

Tomkins is clear that his interests lie not with cognition per se as an idealized, autonomous, executive function but with a cognitive *system* and how it conjoins with affects and drives and scripts (or what he is now calling the motivational system). In *AIC4,* the cognitive system and the motivational system are each understood as just one-half of his human being theory. Moreover, each system has a distinctive function: the cognitive system is primarily involved in the *transformation* of information, whereas the motivational system is primarily involved in the *amplification* of information. However, just as we noted in the first chapter of this book that Tomkins makes a distinction between affects and drives only in the end to claim that such a distinction cannot hold, we note here that this distinction between a cognitive system and a motivational system is valuable for Tomkins precisely because it is unstable. In the first instance, the systems themselves are mosaics— Tomkins just as often refers to a set of cognitive subsystems as he does to a singular cognitive system, and the motivational system is everywhere disassembled into its constituent parts (affects and drives and auxiliary events like pain or reticular activation). In addition, it is common for Tomkins to distinguish between the cognitive system and the motivational system only then to gesture toward their inseparability:

> Because of the high degree of interpenetration and interconnect-
> edness of each part with every other part and with the whole, the
> distinction we have drawn between the cognitive half and the
> motivational half must be considered to be a fragile distinction
> between transformation and amplification as a specialized type
> of transformation. (4:7)

Tomkins's description of these two imbricated halves of mind is exemplary of his predisposition (evident through all four volumes of *AIC*) to
think always in terms of admixture, and it demonstrates the theoretical
acumen that attention to commixture and composition and dislinking
can deliver:

> Cognitions coassembled with affects become hot and urgent.
> Affects coassembled with cognitions become better informed
> and smarter. The major distinction between the two halves is that
> between *amplification* by the motivational system and *transforma-
> tion* by the cognitive system. But the amplified information of
> the motivational system can be and must be transformed by the
> cognitive system, and the transformed information of the cognitive
> system can be and must be amplified by the motivational system.
> **Amplification without transformation would be blind; transfor-
> mation without amplification would be weak. The blind mecha-
> nisms must be given sight; the weak mechanisms must be given
> strength. All information is at once biased and informed.** (4:7)

It seems fair to argue, then, that the ambition of this final volume is not to
turn the reader toward cognition at the expense of a theory of affect but
rather to turn the reader toward the logics of cognitive-motivational dependency, independency, and interdependency that must, for Tomkins,
be the infrastructure of any psychological account of a human being.

The cognitive revolution of the 1960s and 1970s is something of a
double-edged sword for Tomkins. On one hand, it further entrenches
the splintering of psychological theory into increasingly specialized and
isolated subfields and so moves psychological research away from the
holism ("general psychology") that Tomkins embraced under the tute-
lage of Henry Murray and through the mixed methods of the Harvard

Psychological Clinic (see chapter 11). On the other hand, to the extent that this new study of cognition was inspired by work in adjacent fields like artificial intelligence and neurophysiology, consciousness becomes an object of interdisciplinary study in ways that Tomkins finds valuable. This ambivalence about cognition structures the four volumes of *AIC*. The final, posthumous volume of *AIC* was written *before* the first three volumes—sometime in the 1950s, Tomkins recalls (see chapter 12). The first three volumes, then, are something of a detour en route to a comprehensive account of personality (human being theory) to which Tomkins was only able to return in the final years of his life and that he left incomplete. We can note, for example, that the opening rhetoric of volume 4 (e.g., "The introversive conception of thinking as a solitary, inner, autonomous process was, in a fundamental sense, un-American" [4:4]) is not unlike the opening to volume 1 (e.g., "Introversion has not been the preferred mode of functioning for the descendants of the American activist pioneers even when they have chosen to devote their lives to the study of human beings" [1:6]), and in this sense, the four volumes form, not a conventional progression from 1962 to 1992, but a return, or an inversion, or perhaps a particularly extended and productive mode of perseveration.

One of the things that might be noteworthy about this chronology of return or perseveration in *AIC* is that it scrambles orthodox histories of twentieth-century psychology and makes it difficult to place Tomkins in a linear history of research on emotion. In these volumes, the reader doesn't simply move from Freudianism to behaviorism, and from behaviorism to cognitivism and the neurosciences. Twentieth-century psychology can be narrativized as a development from the unconscious to drives to cognition to affect only by significantly reducing the internal contradictions of this intellectual archive—by disregarding the false starts, by ignoring the disagreements that came too early to be heard, and by overlooking the traces of the old paradigm within the new. The scrambled chronologies, feedback loops, loosely structured taxonomies, and repetitions in these four volumes can feel disorienting to a reader, and no doubt all four volumes could be more tightly edited. But we would also like to suggest that Tomkins's duplications and returns signal a theory that doesn't just *describe* coassembly as a psychological principle but also *performs* such rearrangements on the psychological texts it engages. An orderly lineage of theories of emotion across the twentieth century is perhaps the least of Tomkins's intellectual concerns.

We have noted in several places in this book that Tomkins figures the combinatorial character of the affect system as a language (see chapters 2 and 12): affect "is in some respects like a letter of an alphabet in a language, changing in significance as it is assembled with varying other letters to form different words, sentences, paragraphs" (3:66). In his discussion of cognition in the final volume of *AIC,* Tomkins turns to another figure of mind's composite architecture: the neuron. Noting that it is "an extraordinarily complex structure" (4:34), Tomkins uses the neuron to illustrate the "complex interpenetration of structure and function" (4:34) not just in neurological systems but also in cognitive systems, broadly understood. For example, each neuron is both a receiver and transmitter of information, and neuronal circuits are structured by feedback and "multiple simultaneous and interactive processes" (4:37). In short, **the most elementary neurons exhibit all the essential properties of the whole cognitive system . . . the neuron proves to be a cognitive system in miniature"** (4:37–38).

This homology between neurology and mind reminds us of Freud's *Project for a Scientific Psychology,* and in the same way that scholarship on the *Project* has argued for its conceptual perspicacity, we suggest that Tomkins's turn to neurology and cognition isn't an argument for neurological reductionism or determinism. Rather, Tomkins uses the neuron to figure the expansive and inventive character of a cognitive system:

> In summary, the neuron is at once a specialized cognitive medium mechanism that is also a monadic, self-sufficient, local self-governor, whose specialization is achieved by differentially weighting and patterning the shared properties of all cognitive mechanisms into dominant and auxiliary functions. In common with all media mechanisms, the neuron is structurally and functionally redundant, partitioned, regenerative, and equipotential, capable of receiving information, translating it, transforming it (e.g., via summation and averaging), amplifying it (via temporal and spatial summation), transmitting it, storing and reverberating it, correlating it, keeping it distinct, and timing it, and of sending a product as well as transmitting a message, feeding its messages back to itself, and

cross talking with a very large population of neighboring as well as distant neurons. (4:38)

Tomkins uses the neuron to argue that mind cannot be reduced to discrete constituent parts: "the coassembly and fusion of both motivational and cognitive mechanisms is the rule, not the exception" (4:8). He names the higher-order organization that emerges from the combinatorial relations of cognition and motivation a *minding system.* Calling explicitly on the "ancient" term *mind*—drawing on its ambiguity as both a cognitive process and the tendency to care—Tomkins argues that a human being as a minding system "innately 'minds' or cares about what he knows" (4:10).

The *Oxford English Dictionary* records an extensive etymology and set of uses of *mind.* As a verb, it is both transitive (to remember, and also to attend, care for, look after, or be sure or certain, or to intend or heed—exemplified in the recurring directive on the London Underground to "mind the gap") and intransitive (for example, in negative, interrogative, and conditional constructions like "never (you) mind"). As a noun, *mind* covers similar territory: remembrance, recollection, attention, purpose, wish, desire, inclination, tendency, character disposition, and (perhaps most concretely) the seat of awareness, thought, volition, feeling, and memory. In naming the human being a minding system, Tomkins is asking us to mind the gap between cognitive and motivational systems. He is asking us to pay attention to this paradoxical taxonomy of separate systems that are always enmeshed. In addition, it is an important principle of Tomkins's human being theory that it will always be "incomplete and ambiguous" (4:10):

> I will argue that any organized system is inherently ambiguous at its boundaries, whether these boundaries be at the top or at the bottom, at the part of the system or at the whole of the system, at the most elementary particle or at the outer reaches of space at the time of the big bang. (4:9)

Because this figuration of cognition and motivation as subsystems of minding has been argued in part through an engagement with the structure and function of a neuron, Tomkins's work in *AIC4* might be used as a frame for contemporary critical engagements with the neurosciences. For example, because Tomkins's minding system advocates for a science of partially dependent, independent, and interdependent subsystems from which nothing can be excluded (e.g., sociality, signification), we could argue for a different set of relations between the affects and neurophysiology. The conjunction affect–neuron might be an opportunity not to subsume psychology to the brain but rather to figure neurology itself as mindful, attentive, and wishful. So when we seek to bring clinical or humanistic arguments into play with the neurosciences, rather than looking for correspondence between affective and neuronal claims, we could be looking to build minding systems of loosely matching and mismatching conceptual components.

In this regard, we are reminded, again, of Freud, specifically, his taxonomies of unconscious, preconscious, conscious and id, ego, superego. Postulated twenty years apart, these two systems occupy a disconcerting relation to each other in the Freudian oeuvre: they neither map neatly onto each other (the id is not the same kind of mental structure as the unconscious; the ego and the conscious describe different kinds of psychic topographies), nor is it the case that the second taxonomy of mind (id, ego, and superego) completely reforms or replaces the first (unconscious, preconscious, conscious). Instead, these two metapsychological systems stand in a conceptual tension in Freud's work, suggesting that minding systems are best theorized as variable, overlapping, resistant to substitution or the logics of linear conceptual progress. So too with Tomkins's coassembly of cognition and motivation: it prepares us to envisage a science of mind that does not just tolerate but perhaps also enjoys mismatching, perseveration, repetitions, and the fusion of its central variables. If the relation between cognitions and affects and drives and neurology and scripts and socialities remains ambiguous (and perhaps unresolvable), we suspect this is the state of mind that Tomkins would like us to heed.

FURTHER READING

Readers wishing to get a general overview of the "cognitive revolution" with which Tomkins is engaging in *AIC4* might want to consult Howard Gardner's *The Mind's New Science: A History of the Cognitive*

Revolution. For an excellent reading of the affect of surprise in scientific research that draws on Tomkins's work, we refer readers to Mike Fortun's "What Toll Pursuit: Affective Assemblages in Genomics and Postgenomics."

The first topography of mind in Freud (conscious, preconscious, unconscious) can be found in *The Interpretation of Dreams* and "The Unconscious." The second topography (id, ego, superego) can be found in *The Ego and the Id*. We relied on Elizabeth A. Wilson's *Neural Geographies* for our account of Freud's *Project for a Scientific Psychology* and contemporary neuroscience.

ACKNOWLEDGMENTS

This project came out of conversations we had about ten years ago that took place between sessions at meetings of the Society for Literature, Science, and the Arts (SLSA). We couldn't help but notice the lively interest in affect at these meetings. No doubt, scholars interested in the conjunction of literature and science and art were finding opportunities to think about the affects in new and compelling ways. But we noted a certain narrowness in how these panels approached questions of affectivity: there was extensive use of Deleuzian and Whiteheadian frameworks and the distinct absence of speakers taking up Tomkins's thinking. We were concerned that the so-called affective turn was leaving out what struck us as a valuable resource for cogent critical and political thought. Because we had each (separately) taught Tomkins's theories in the classroom and used them in our research, we realized the significant challenge involved in making his work legible and comprehensible for audiences in the humanities and social sciences. We decided to pursue this *Handbook* as something like a translation project so as to make Tomkins's thinking more accessible to our students, our colleagues, and scholars in other fields.

Thanks, first, to Richard Morrison, former editorial director at the University of Minnesota Press, who expressed great enthusiasm for the project. We are grateful to Jason Weidemann, the current editorial director, for his support and to Leah Pennywark, Holly Monteith, and Rachel Moeller for shepherding the project to completion. Lisa Blackman and Felicity Callard provided reader reports to the press that we found helpful in our final revisions.

We are very grateful to the staff at the Archives of the History of American Psychology, at the Drs. Nicholas and Dorothy Cummings Center for the History of Psychology, University of Akron, for assistance with their extensive holdings of Tomkins materials. We also thank the staff who helped us access materials at the Harvard University Archives (Henry A. Murray Papers), the Center for the History of Medicine at the Francis A. Countway Library of Medicine, Harvard

University (Edward Bibring Papers), the Office of the President Records at Princeton University, and the University Archives and Records Center at the University of Pennsylvania.

Lauren Abramson, Lauren Berlant, Sean McAlister, Michael Moon, and Ada Smailbegović encouraged our work on this project. We're grateful for their support. Ingrid Meintjes did beautiful work as a research assistant, Peta Shera (miraculously) tracked down all Tomkins's published works, and Samantha Wrisley provided invaluable help in preparing the final manuscript. Sarah McKee supported the process of making this book available open access through Emory University's initiative for Digital Publishing in the Humanities, which is funded by the Andrew W. Mellon Foundation and housed in the Bill and Carol Fox Center for Humanistic Inquiry. The University of British Columbia Scholarly Publication Fund offered assistance for indexing and permissions.

Adam thanks the graduate students in several iterations of his Affect Theory, Materialist Criticism seminar at the University of British Columbia for thinking so deftly with Tomkins's ideas vis-à-vis literary and theoretical texts, films, comics, and other media. He also thanks participants in A Biocultural Hinge: Theorizing Affect and Emotion across Disciplines (May 1–4, 2013), an International Roundtable Discussion co-organized with Shelly Rosenblum (curator of academic programs at the Morris and Helen Belkin Art Gallery) and supported by the Peter Wall Institute for Advanced Studies at the University of British Columbia, Vancouver. He is grateful to Gretty Mirdal for an invitation to present material from this book to the Brain, Culture, and Society group at the Institut d'études avancées de Paris, where he held a residential fellowship during 2018–19. He happily acknowledges the institute for its support during the time he completed chapter revisions. And, as always, he thanks Marguerite Pigeon for sustaining with him the muddle of positive and negative affect that is a long-term partnership or marriage.

It was in a Sydney-based Tomkins reading group, formed in the wake of *Shame and Its Sisters,* that Elizabeth first read her way carefully through Tomkins's remarkable writing and encountered the strong feelings of identification, interest, and enjoyment that it can generate. She is grateful to Maria Angel, Susan Best, Anna Gibbs, Melissa Hardie, Doris McIlwain, and Gillian Straker for this joint reading enterprise. She thanks everyone who participated in the 2016–17 Mellon-funded

Sawyer Seminar (New Scholarship on the Affects) at Emory University as well as the graduate students in classes at Emory (on the affective turn; on theories of mind; and on theories of affect, attachment, and intersubjectivity) who struggled along with her to make sense of Tomkins's expansive and sometimes formidable texts. Her colleagues Carla Freeman, Lynne Huffer, and Michael Moon have been wonderful interlocutors on questions of affect for many years. Ashley Shelden made affectivity matter the most.

We would like to thank each other for the surprising, delightful experience of collaborating on this book, surprising because so often more enjoyable than expected. Strange to say, it's actually been fun to think and write about Tomkins together. This project has given us the chance to develop and fine-tune our understanding of challenging material, to compare notes, and to test ideas in collusion. Writing as two is a much less lonely business than writing as one.

Finally, thanks to Eve Kosofsky Sedgwick for introducing us to Tomkins's writing in the first place. For one of us, reading the four volumes of *AIC* with Eve turned Tomkins into a lifelong companion. For the other, coming to Tomkins's work through Eve's exceptional readings greatly expanded her horizons. We dedicate this book to her.

CHRONOLOGY OF TOMKINS'S LIFE AND WORK

In constructing this chronology, we consulted *Exploring Affect: The Selected Writings of Silvan S. Tomkins,* edited by E. Virginia Demos; "Silvan S. Tomkins: A Biographical Sketch" by Irving Alexander, in *Shame and Its Sisters: A Silvan Tomkins Reader,* edited by Eve Kosofsky Sedgwick and Adam Frank; the biographical information presented on the Tomkins Institute website (http://www.tomkins.org/); and archival materials (university transcripts, census data, marriage records, correspondence).

1911: Born June 4 in Philadelphia to Russian Jewish immigrant parents, Samuel Solomon Tomkins, a dentist, and Rose Tomkins (née Novak). Grew up in Camden, New Jersey. Sister Charlotte born two years later.

1927–30: BA, University of Pennsylvania. Takes courses primarily in English, philosophy, and psychology; concentrates on playwriting.

1930–34: MA and PhD in philosophy, University of Pennsylvania. Dissertation: "Conscience, Self Love and Benevolence in the System of Bishop Butler," supervised by Professor Louis W. Flaccus. Takes courses with Edgar A. Singer Jr.

1934–35: Hired by a racing syndicate in New Jersey to handicap horse races, nicknamed "The Professor." Continues to play the horses in Atlantic City and Miami Beach for several years.

1935–37: Postdoctoral fellow in philosophy at Harvard University. Works with Willard Van Orman Quine, Ralph Barton Perry, Henry Sheffer, and (possibly) Alfred North Whitehead. Brief marriage to Mary Shoemaker.

1937–43: Moves to the Harvard Psychological Clinic as a postdoctoral fellow; later becomes a research assistant. Works with Henry A. Murray and Robert W. White on studies of personality. With Daniel Horn, devises the Tomkins–Horn Picture Arrangement Test (PAT). Enters a seven-year psychoanalysis with Ruth Burr. Dedicates *Contemporary Psychopathology: A Sourcebook* (1943) to Burr.

1943–46: Instructor, Department of Psychology, Harvard University. Marries Elizabeth (BeeGee) Taylor.

1946–47: Lecturer, Department of Social Relations, Harvard University. Publishes *The Thematic Apperception Test: The Theory and Technique of Interpretation* (1947) in collaboration with Elizabeth Tomkins.

1947–55: Visiting professor, Department of Psychology, Princeton University. Appointed associate professor and director of clinical training program (1949). Works with the Educational Testing Service. Serves as consultant at Fort Dix, the Pennsylvania Psychiatric Institute, and the National Institute of Mental Health. First presentations on affect theory (1951, 1954) published in *La Psychoanalyse* (1956), edited by Jacques Lacan. Birth of son Mark Tomkins (1955).

1955–64: Professor, Department of Psychology, and director of clinical training program, Princeton University. Invited to spend a year (1960–61) as a research fellow at the Center for Advanced Study in the Behavioral Sciences, Stanford University, where he completes the first two volumes of *Affect Imagery Consciousness*. Experiences serious injury while surfing in Hawai'i (1961). Publishes *AIC: Volume 1. The Positive Affects* (1962) and *AIC: Volume 2. The Negative Affects* (1963). Receives Career Scientist Award from the National Institute of Mental Health (1964).

1964–68: Research professor and director of the Center for Research in Cognition and Affect, Graduate Center, City University of New York. Develops research on smoking and addiction, the psychology of knowledge, affect and faciality, and other subjects.

1968–76: Research professor, Department of Psychology at Livingston College, Rutgers University. Marriage with BeeGee ends. Retires from Rutgers as emeritus professor.

1980–91: Adjunct professor, Busch Center, University of Pennsylvania. Presentations and publications on script theory. Diagnosed with lymphoma (1990); sees the publication of *AIC: Volume 3. The Negative Affects: Anger and Fear* (1991). Dies June 10, 1991 (age eighty-one), at Shore Memorial Hospital in New Jersey. *AIC: Volume 4. Cognition: Duplication and Transformation of Information* published the following year.

BIBLIOGRAPHY OF TOMKINS'S PUBLISHED WRITINGS

In constructing this bibliography, we consulted *Exploring Affect: The Selected Writings of Silvan S. Tomkins,* edited by E. Virginia Demos; the bibliographical information on the Tomkins Institute website (http://www.tomkins.org/); and the Silvan Tomkins Papers at the Drs. Nicholas and Dorothy Cummings Center for the History of Psychology, University of Akron.

1934

Tomkins, Silvan. "Conscience, Self Love and Benevolence in the System of Bishop Butler." PhD diss., University of Pennsylvania.

1943

Tomkins, Silvan. "An Analysis of the Use of Electric Shock with Human Subjects." *Journal of Psychology* 15, no. 2: 285–97.

Tomkins, Silvan. "Experimental Study of Anxiety." *Journal of Psychology* 15, no. 2: 307–13.

Gerbrands, Henry, and Silvan Tomkins. "An Apparatus for the Study of Motor Learning under Threat of Electric Shock." *Journal of Psychology* 15, no. 2: 299–305.

Tomkins, Silvan, ed. *Contemporary Psychopathology: A Source Book.* Cambridge, Mass.: Harvard University Press.

1945

White, Robert, Silvan Tomkins, and Thelma Alper. "The Realistic Synthesis: A Personality Study." *Journal of Abnormal and Social Psychology* 40, no. 2: 228–48.

1947

Tomkins, Silvan, with Elizabeth Tomkins. *The Thematic Apperception Test: The Theory and Technique of Interpretation.* New York: Grune and Stratton.

1949

Tomkins, Silvan. "The Present Status of the Thematic Apperception Test." *American Journal of Orthopsychiatry* 19, no. 2: 358–62.

1950

Tomkins, Silvan. "Personality and Intelligence: Integration of Projective and Psychometric Techniques." In *Relation of Psychological Tests to Psychiatry,* edited by Paul Zubin and Joseph Zubin, 87–104. New York: Grune and Stratton.

1951

Tomkins, Silvan. "A Discussion of 'Personality Structures and Personality Measurement' of R. B. Cattell." In *1951 Invitational Testing Conference,* 97–107. Princeton, N.J.: Educational Testing Service.

1952

Tomkins, Silvan. "The Tomkins–Horn Picture-Arrangement Test." *Transactions of the New York Academy of Science* 15, no. 2, ser. II: 46–50.

1955

Tomkins, Silvan. "Consciousness and the Unconscious in a Model of the Human Being." In *Proceedings of the Fourteenth International Congress of Psychology: Montreal—June 1954. Actes du Quatorzième Congrès International de Psychologie,* 160–61. Amsterdam: North-Holland.

Tomkins, Silvan. "The Role of Tests in the United States with Particular Reference to the Tomkins–Horn Picture Arrangement Test." In *Actas del Primer Congreso Interamericano de Psicología,* 218–23. Ciudad Turjillo, Republica Dominicana: Editoria Del Caribe.

Tomkins, Silvan, and John Miner. "Contributions to the Standardization of the Tomkins–Horn Picture Arrangement Test: Plate Norms." *Journal of Psychology* 39, no. 1: 199–214.

1956

Tomkins, Silvan S. "La Conscience et L'Inconscient Représentés dans un Modèle de L'Être Humain." In *La Psychoanalyse. 1. Travaux des Années 1953–1955,* translated by Muriel Cahen, edited by Jacques Lacan, 275–86. Paris: Presses Universitaires de France.

1957

Tomkins, Silvan. "The Influence of Sigmund Freud on American Culture." In *The Influence of John Locke and Sigmund Freud on American Culture,* 1–52. Princeton University Special Program in American Civilization Conference. Princeton, N.J.: Princeton University Press.

Tomkins, Silvan, and John Miner. *The Tomkins–Horn Picture Arrangement Test.* New York: Springer.

1958

Tomkins, Silvan. Foreword to *The Negro Personality: A Rigorous Investigation of the Effects of Culture,* by Bertram Karon. New York: Springer.

Reed, Charles, Irving Alexander, and Silvan Tomkins, eds. *Psychopathology: A Source Book.* Cambridge, Mass.: Harvard University Press.

1959

Tomkins, Silvan, and John Miner. *PAT Interpretation: Scope and Technique.* New York: Springer.

1960

Tomkins, Silvan. "Personality Research and Psychopathology: A Commentary." In *Perspectives in Personality Research,* edited by Henry David and J. C. Brengelmann, 150–58. New York: Springer.

1961

Tomkins, Silvan. "Discussion of Dr. Holt's Paper." In *Contemporary Issues in Thematic Apperceptive Methods,* edited by Jerome Kagan and Gerald Lesser, 44–50. Springfield, Ill.: Charles Thomas.

McCarter, Robert, Silvan Tomkins, and Harold Schiffman. "Early Recollections as Predictors of Tomkins–Horn Picture Arrangement Performance." *Journal of Individual Psychology* 17, no. 2: 177–80.

1962

Tomkins, Silvan. *Affect Imagery Consciousness. Volume 1. The Positive Affects. New York:* Springer.

Tomkins, Silvan. "Commentary: The Ideology of Research Strategies." In *Measurement in Personality and Cognition,* edited by Samuel Messick and John Ross, 285–94. *New York:* John Wiley.

1963

Tomkins, Silvan. *Affect Imagery Consciousness. Volume 2. The Negative Affects. New York:* Springer.

Tomkins, Silvan. "Left and Right: A Basic Dimension of Ideology and Personality." In *The Study of Lives: Essays on Personality in Honor of Henry A. Murray,* edited by Robert White, 389–411. New York: Atherton.

Tomkins, Silvan. "Simulation of Personality: The Interrelationships between Affect, Memory, Thinking, Perception, and Action." In *Computer Simulation and Personality: Frontier of Psychological Theory,* edited by Silvan Tomkins and Samuel Messick, 3–57. New York: John Wiley.

Dyer, Henry, Silvan Tomkins, Ralph Turner, and Sherwood Washburn. *Race and Intelligence*. Edited by Melvin Tumin. New York: Anti-Defamation League of B'nai B'rith.

Tomkins, Silvan, and Samuel Messick, eds. *Computer Simulation of Personality: Frontier of Psychological Theory.* New York: John Wiley.

1964

Tomkins, Silvan. *Polarity Scale.* New York: Springer.

Rosenhan, David, and Silvan Tomkins. "On Preference for Hypnosis and Hypnotizability." *International Journal of Clinical and Experimental Hypnosis* 12, no. 2: 109–14.

Tomkins, Silvan, and Robert McCarter. "What and Where Are the Primary Affects? Some Evidence for a Theory." *Perceptual and Motor Skills* 18, no. 1: 119–58.

1965

Tomkins, Silvan. "Affect and the Psychology of Knowledge." In *Affect, Cognition and Personality: Empirical Studies,* edited by Silvan Tomkins and Carroll Izard, 72–97. New York: Springer.

Tomkins, Silvan. "The Biopsychosociality of the Family." In *Aspects of the Analysis of Family Structure,* edited by Ansley Coale, Lloyd Fallers, Marion Levy, David Schneider, and Silvan Tomkins, 102–248. Princeton, N.J.: Princeton University Press.

Tomkins, Silvan. "The Psychology of Being Right and Left." *Transaction* 3, no. 1: 23–27.

Tomkins, Silvan. "The Psychology of Commitment. Part 1: The Constructive Role of Violence and Suffering for the Individual and for His Society." In *Affect, Cognition, and Personality: Empirical Studies,* edited by Silvan Tomkins and Carroll Izard, 148–71. New York: Springer.

Tomkins, Silvan. "The Psychology of Commitment. Part 2: Reactions to the Assassination of President Kennedy." In *Affect, Cognition, and Personality: Empirical Studies,* edited by Silvan Tomkins and Carroll Izard, 172–97. New York: Springer.

Tomkins, Silvan. "The Psychology of Commitment: The Constructive Role of Violence and Suffering for the Individual and His Society." In *The Antislavery Vanguard: New Essays on the Abolitionists,* edited by Martin Duberman, 270–98. Princeton, N.J.: Princeton University Press.

Coale, Ansley, Lloyd Fallers, Marion Levy, David Schneider, and Silvan Tomkins, eds. *Aspects of the Analysis of Family Structure.* Princeton, N.J.: Princeton University Press.

Tomkins, Silvan, and Carroll Izard, eds. *Affect, Cognition, and Personality: Empirical Studies.* New York: Springer.

1966

Tomkins, Silvan. Foreword to *Daydreaming: An Introduction to the Experimental Study of Inner Experience,* by Jerome L. Singer. New York: Random House.

Tomkins, Silvan. "Projective Technique." *Psychology Quarterly* 2, no. 2: 1–4.

Tomkins, Silvan. "Psychological Model for Smoking Behavior." *American Journal of Public Health* 56, no. 12: 17–20.

Tomkins, Silvan. "Theoretical Implications and Guidelines to Future Research." In *Behavioral Aspects to Smoking: A Conference Report,* edited by Bernard Mausner and Ellen H. Platt. *Health Education Monographs,* Suppl. 2: 35–48.

Izard, Carroll, and Silvan Tomkins. "Affect and Behavior: Anxiety as a Negative Affect." In *Anxiety and Behavior,* edited by Charles D. Spielberger, 81–125. New York: Academic Press.

1967

Tomkins, Silvan. "Homo Patiens: A Reexamination of the Concept of Drive." In *Challenges of Humanistic Psychology,* edited by James F. T. Bugenthal, 53–59. New York: McGraw-Hill.

Tomkins, Silvan. "Psychology of Smoking." *Psychology Quarterly* 2, no. 3: 11–13.

1968

Tomkins, Silvan. "Affects: Primary Motives of Man." *Humanitas* 3, no. 3: 321–45.

Tomkins, Silvan. "A Modified Model of Smoking Behavior." In *Smoking, Health, and Behavior,* edited by Edgar Borgatta and Robert Evans, 165–86. Chicago: Aldine.

Tomkins, Silvan. "Psychological Model for Smoking Behavior." *Review of Existential Psychology and Psychiatry* 8, no. 1: 28–33.

Tomkins, Silvan. "Some Varieties of Psychological Organization." In *The Reach of Mind: Essays in Memory of Kurt Goldstein,* edited by Marianne Simmel, 219–30. New York: Springer.

1969

Tomkins, Silvan. "Free Will and the Degrees-of-Freedom Principle." In *William James: Unfinished Business,* edited by Robert MacLeod, 103–6. Washington, D.C.: American Psychological Association.

Tomkins, Silvan. "Interrelationships of Different Measures of Affect." *Psychology Quarterly* 3, no. 4: 1–5.

Tomkins, Silvan. Introduction to *Psychoanalysis: Radical and Conservative*, by Philip Lichtenberg. New York: Springer.

Tomkins, Silvan. "Personality Theory and Social Science." In *Interdisciplinary Relationships in the Social Sciences*, edited by Muzafer Sherif and Carolyn Sherif, 197–208. Chicago: Aldine.

Suedfeld, Peter, Silvan Tomkins, and William Tucker. "On Relations among Perceptual and Cognitive Measures of Information Processing." *Perception and Psycho-physics* 6, no. 1: 45–46.

1970

Tomkins, Silvan. Foreword to *Social Change and the Individual: Japan before and after Defeat in World War II*, by Kazuko Tsurumi. Princeton, N.J.: Princeton University Press.

1971

Tomkins, Silvan. "Homo Patiens." In *Personality Theory and Information Processing*, edited by Harold Schroder and Peter Suedfeld, 209–39. New York: Ronald Press.

Tomkins, Silvan. "Ideological Conflicts about the Nature of Risk-Taking." In *Risk-Taking Behavior: Concepts, Methods, and Applications to Smoking and Drug Abuse*, edited by Richard Carney, 182–92. Springfield, Ill.: Charles Thomas.

Tomkins, Silvan. "A Theory of Memory." In *Cognition and Affect*, edited by John Antrobus, 59–130. Boston: Little, Brown.

Tomkins, Silvan. "A Theory of Risk-Taking Behavior." In *Risk-Taking Behavior: Concepts, Methods, and Applications to Smoking and Drug Abuse*, edited by Richard Carney, 19–24. Springfield, Ill.: Charles Thomas.

Ekman, Paul, Wallace Friesen, and Silvan Tomkins. "Facial Affect Scoring Technique: A First Validity Study." *Semiotica* 3, no. 1: 37–58.

1972

Tomkins, Silvan. "Comments on Dr. Izard's Paper." In *Anxiety: Current Trends in Theory and Research*, vol. 1, edited by Charles Spielberger, 107–12. New York: Academic Press.

1973

Ikard, Frederick, and Silvan Tomkins. "The Experience of Affect as a Determinant of Smoking Behavior." *Journal of Abnormal Psychology* 81, no. 2: 172–81.

1975

Tomkins, Silvan. "The Phantasy behind the Face." *Journal of Personality Assessment* 39, no. 6: 550–62.

1976

Atwood, George, and Silvan Tomkins. "On the Subjectivity of Personality Theory." *Journal of the History of the Behavioral Sciences* 12, no. 2: 166–77.

1979

Tomkins, Silvan. "Script Theory: Differential Magnification of Affects." In *Nebraska Symposium on Motivation—1978,* vol. 26, edited by Herbert Howe and Richard Dienstbier, 201–36. Lincoln: University of Nebraska Press.

1980

Tomkins, Silvan. "Affect as Amplification: Some Modifications in Theory." In *Emotion: Theory, Research, and Experience,* edited by Robert Plutchik and Henry Kellerman, 141–64. New York: Academic Press.

Tomkins, Silvan. Introduction to *Shame: The Power of Caring,* edited by Gershen Kaufman. Rochester, Vt.: Schenkman.

1981

Tomkins, Silvan. "The Quest for Primary Motives: Biography and Autobiography of an Idea." *Journal of Personality and Social Psychology* 41, no. 2: 306–29.

Tomkins, Silvan. "The Rise, Fall, and Resurrection of the Study of Personality." *Journal of Mind and Behavior* 2, no. 4: 443–52.

Tomkins, Silvan. "The Role of Facial Response in the Experience of Emotion: A Reply to Tourangeau and Ellsworth." *Journal of Personality and Social Psychology* 40, no. 2: 355–57.

1982

Tomkins, Silvan. "Affect Theory." In *Emotion in the Human Face,* 2nd ed., edited by Paul Ekman, 353–95. Cambridge: Cambridge University Press.

Tomkins, Silvan. "Personology Is a Complex, Lifelong, Never-Ending Enterprise." *Personality and Social Psychology Bulletin* 8, no. 4: 608–11.

1984

Tomkins, Silvan. "Affect Theory." In *Approaches to Emotion,* edited by Klaus Scherer and Paul Ekman, 163–95. Hillsdale, N.J.: Lawrence Erlbaum.

1987

Tomkins, Silvan. "Script Theory." In *The Emergence of Personality,* edited by Joel Aronoff, Albert Rabin, and Robert Zucker, 147–216. New York: Springer.

Tomkins, Silvan. "Shame." In *The Many Faces of Shame,* edited by Donald L. Nathanson, 133–61. New York: Guilford Press.

1988

Mosher, Donald, and Silvan Tomkins. "Scripting the Macho Man: Hypermasculine Socialization and Enculturation." *Journal of Sex Research* 25, no. 1: 60–84.

1991

Tomkins, Silvan. *Affect Imagery Consciousness: Volume 3. The Negative Affects: Anger and Fear.* New York: Springer.

1992

Tomkins, Silvan. *Affect Imagery Consciousness: Volume 4. Cognition: Duplication and Transformation of Information.* New York: Springer.

1995

Tomkins, Silvan. "Inverse Archeology: Facial Affect and the Interfaces of Scripts within and between Persons." In *Exploring Affect: The Selected Writings of Silvan S. Tomkins,* edited by E. Virginia Demos, 284–90. Cambridge: Cambridge University Press.

REFERENCES

Alexander, Irving. "Ideology as Part of the Tomkins Legacy." In *Exploring Affect: The Selected Writings of Silvan S. Tomkins,* ed. E. Virginia Demos, 101–5. Cambridge: Cambridge University Press, 1995.

Alexander, Irving. "Silvan S. Tomkins: A Biographical Sketch." In *Shame and Its Sisters: A Silvan Tomkins Reader,* ed. Eve Kosofsky Sedgwick and Adam Frank, 251–63. Durham, N.C.: Duke University Press, 1995.

Allport, Gordon. "The Ego in Contemporary Psychology." *Psychological Review* 50, no. 5 (1943): 451–78.

Allport, Gordon. *The Person in Psychology: Selected Essays.* Boston: Beacon Press, 1968.

Anderson, James William. "An Interview with Henry A. Murray on His Meeting with Sigmund Freud." *Psychoanalytic Psychology* 34, no. 3 (2017): 322–31.

Ashton, Vicki, and James Dwyer. "The Left: Lateral Eye Movements and Ideology." *Perceptual and Motor Skills* 41, no. 1 (1975): 248–50.

Atwood, George, and Silvan Tomkins. "On the Subjectivity of Personality Theory." *Journal of the History of the Behavioral Sciences* 12, no. 2 (1976): 166–77.

Barad, Karen. *Meeting the Universe Halfway: Quantum Physics and the Entanglement of Matter and Meaning.* Durham, N.C.: Duke University Press, 2007.

Barrett, Lisa Feldman. "Construction as an Integrative Framework for the Science of the Emotion." In *The Psychological Construction of Emotion,* edited by Lisa Feldman Barrett and James A. Russell, 448–58. New York: Guilford Press, 2015.

Beer, Gillian. *Darwin's Plots: Evolutionary Narrative in Darwin, George Eliot and Nineteenth-Century Fiction.* Cambridge: Cambridge University Press, 1983.

Bennett, Jane. *Vibrant Matter: A Political Ecology of Things.* Durham, N.C.: Duke University Press, 2010.

Blackman, Lisa. *Immaterial Bodies: Affect, Embodiment, Mediation.* London: Sage, 2013.

Blackman, Lisa, and Couze Venn, eds. "Affect." Special issue. *Body and Society* 16, no. 1 (2010).

Boring, Edwin. "Was This Analysis a Success?" *Journal of Abnormal and Social Psychology* 35, no. 1 (1940): 4–10.

Boucher, Wayne. *Spinoza in English: A Bibliography from the Seventeenth Century to the Present.* Leiden, Netherlands: E. J. Brill, 1991.

Carlson, Rae, and Julie Brincka. "Studies in Script Theory: III. Ideology and Political Imagination." *Political Psychology* 8, no. 4 (1987): 563–74.

Clough, Patricia Ticineto. *The Affective Turn: Theorizing the Social.* Durham, N.C.: Duke University Press, 2007.

Damasio, Antonio. *Looking for Spinoza: Joy, Sorrow, and the Feeling Brain.* New York: Harcourt, 2003.

Darwin, Charles. *The Expression of the Emotions in Man and Animals.* 1872. Reprint, Chicago: University of Chicago Press, 1965.

Daston, Lorraine, and Peter Galison. *Objectivity.* New York: Zone Books, 2008.

Deleuze, Gilles. *Expressionism in Philosophy: Spinoza.* Translated by Martin Joughin. New York: Zone Books, 1990.

Deleuze, Gilles. *Spinoza: Practical Philosophy.* Translated by Robert Hurley. San Francisco: City Lights Books, 1988.

Demos, Virginia. *The Affect Theory of Silvan Tomkins for Psychoanalysis and Psychotherapy: Recasting the Essentials.* London: Routledge, 2019.

Demos, Virginia, ed. *Exploring Affect: The Selected Writings of Silvan S. Tomkins.* Cambridge: Cambridge University Press, 1995.

Dharwadker, Vinay. "Emotion in Motion: The Nātyaśhāstra, Darwin, and Affect Theory." *PMLA* 130, no. 5 (2015): 1381–1404.

Dick, Phillip K. *Do Androids Dream of Electric Sheep?* 1968. Reprint, New York: Ballantine Books, 1996.

Edelman, Gerald. *Bright Air, Brilliant Fire: On the Matter of the Mind.* New York: Basic Books, 1992.

Edelman, Gerald. *The Remembered Present: A Biological Theory of Consciousness.* New York: Basic Books, 1989.

Ekman, Paul. "Afterword. Universality of Emotional Expression? A Personal History of the Dispute." In *The Expression of the Emotions in Man and Animals,* by Charles Darwin, 363–93. Oxford: Oxford University Press, 1998.

Ekman, Paul. *Darwin and Facial Expression: A Century of Research in Review.* Cambridge, Mass.: Academic Press, 1973.

Ekman, Paul, ed. *Emotion in the Human Face.* Cambridge: Cambridge University Press, 1982.

Ekman, Paul. *Emotions Revealed: Recognizing Faces and Feelings to Improve Communication and Emotional Life.* New York: Times Books, 2003.

Ekman, Paul. *What the Face Reveals: Basic and Applied Studies of Spontaneous Expression Using the Facial Action Coding System (FACS).* 1997. Reprint, Oxford: Oxford University Press, 2003.

Ekman, Paul, and Daniel Cordaro. "What Is Meant by Calling Emotions Basic." *Emotion Review* 3, no. 4 (2011): 364–70.

Ekman, Paul, and Richard J. Davidson, eds. *The Nature of Emotion: Fundamental Questions.* Oxford: Oxford University Press, 1994.

Ekman, Paul, Wallace Friesen, and Silvan Tomkins. "Facial Affect Scoring Technique: A First Validity Study." *Semiotica* 3, no. 1 (1971): 37–58.

Emerson, Ralph Waldo. *The Collected Works of Ralph Waldo Emerson.* 7 vols. Introduction and notes by Robert E. Spiller. Cambridge, Mass.: Belknap Press, 1971–2013.

Feuer, Lewis S. *Varieties of Scientific Experience: Emotive Aims in Scientific Hypotheses.* New Brunswick, N.J.: Transaction, 1995.

Fitzgerald, Des, and Felicity Callard. "Social Science and Neuroscience beyond Interdisciplinarity: Experimental Entanglements." *Theory, Culture, and Society* 32, no. 1 (2015): 3–32.

Forrester, John. *Thinking in Cases.* Cambridge: Polity Press, 2017.

Fortun, Mike. "What Toll Pursuit: Affective Assemblages in Genomics and Postgenomics." In *Postgenomics: Perspectives on Biology after the Genome,* edited by Sarah S. Richardson and Hallam Stevens, 32–55. Durham, N.C.: Duke University Press, 2015.

Frank, Adam. "Phantoms Limn: Silvan Tomkins and Affective Prosthetics." *Theory and Psychology* 17, no. 4 (2007): 515–28.

Frank, Adam. "Some Affective Bases for Guilt: Tomkins, Freud, Object Relations." *ESC: English Studies in Canada* 32, no. 1 (2006): 11–25.

Frank, Adam. "Some Avenues for Feeling." *Criticism* 46, no. 3 (2004): 511–24.

Frank, Adam, and Elizabeth A. Wilson. "Like-minded." *Critical Inquiry* 38, no. 4 (2012): 870–77.

Freud, Sigmund. "The Ego and the Id." In *The Standard Edition of the Complete Psychological Works of Sigmund Freud: Volume XIX. 1923–1925,* edited by James Strachey, 3–66. London: Hogarth Press, 1923.

Freud, Sigmund. "Instincts and Their Vicissitudes." In *The Standard Edition of the Complete Psychological Works of Sigmund Freud: Volume XIV. 1914–1916,* edited by James Strachey, 108–40. London: Hogarth Press, 1915.

Freud, Sigmund. "The Interpretation of Dreams." In *The Standard Edition of the Complete Psychological Works of Sigmund Freud: Volume IV. 1900,* edited by James Strachey. London: Hogarth Press, 1900.

Freud, Sigmund. "Repression." In *The Standard Edition of the Complete*

Psychological Works of Sigmund Freud: Volume XIV. 1914–1916, edited by James Strachey, 141–58. London: Hogarth Press, 1915.

Freud, Sigmund. "Three Essays on the Theory of Sexuality." In *The Standard Edition of the Complete Psychological Works of Sigmund Freud: Volume VII. 1901–1905,* edited by James Strachey, 123–245. London: Hogarth Press, 1905.

Freud, Sigmund. "The Unconscious." In *The Standard Edition of the Complete Psychological Works of Sigmund Freud: Volume XIV. 1914–1916,* edited by James Strachey, 159–215. London: Hogarth Press, 1915.

Freud, Sigmund, and Josef Breuer. "Studies on Hysteria." In *The Standard Edition of the Complete Psychological Works of Sigmund Freud: Volume II. 1893–1895,* edited by James Strachey. London: Hogarth Press, 1895.

Frois-Wittmann, Jean. "The Judgment of Facial Expression." *Journal of Experimental Psychology* 13, no. 2 (1930): 113–51.

Fullerton, George Stuart. *The Philosophy of Spinoza.* New York: Henry Holt, 1892.

Galison, Peter. "The Ontology of the Enemy: Norbert Wiener and the Cybernetic Vision." *Critical Inquiry* 21, no. 1 (1994): 228–66.

Gardner, Howard. *The Mind's New Science: A History of the Cognitive Revolution.* New York: Basic Books, 1987.

Gendron, Maria, and Lisa Feldman Barrett. "Reconstructing the Past: A Century of Ideas about Emotion in Psychology." *Emotion Review* 1, no. 4 (2009): 316–39.

Geoghegan, Bernard Dionysius. "From Information Theory to French Theory: Jakobson, Lévi-Strauss, and the Cybernetic Apparatus." *Critical Inquiry* 38, no. 1 (2011): 96–126.

Gerbrands, Henry, and Silvan Tomkins. "An Apparatus for the Study of Motor Learning under Threat of Electric Shock." *Journal of Psychology* 15, no. 2 (1943): 299–305.

Gladwell, Malcolm. "The Naked Face." *New Yorker,* August 5, 2002, 38–49.

Green, André. *The Fabric of Affect in the Psychoanalytic Discourse.* London: Routledge, 1999.

Gregg, Melissa, and Gregory J. Seigworth, eds. *The Affect Theory Reader.* Durham, N.C.: Duke University Press, 2010.

Gregg, Melissa, and Gregory J. Seigworth. "An Inventory of Shimmers." In *The Affect Theory Reader,* edited by Melissa Gregg and Gregory J. Seigworth, 1–25. Durham, N.C.: Duke University Press, 2010.

Hayles, N. Katherine. *How We Became Posthuman.* Chicago: Chicago University Press, 1999.

Heims, Steve Joshua. *The Cybernetics Group.* Cambridge, Mass.: MIT Press, 1991.

Hemmings, Clare. "Invoking Affect: Cultural Theory and the Ontological Turn." *Cultural Studies* 19, no. 5 (2005): 548–67.

Ikard, Frederick, and Silvan Tomkins. "The Experience of Affect as a Determinant of Smoking Behavior." *Journal of Abnormal Psychology* 81, no. 2 (1973): 172–81.

Israel, Jonathan. *Radical Enlightenment: Philosophy and the Making of Modernity.* Oxford: Oxford University Press, 2001.

Jacquette, Dale, ed. *Philosophy, Psychology, and Psychologism.* Dordrecht, Netherlands: Kluwer Academic, 2003.

Jacquette, Dale. "Psychologism the Philosophical Shibboleth." *Philosophy and Rhetoric* 30, no. 3 (1997): 312–31.

James, William. *The Correspondence of William James.* 12 vols. Edited by Ignas K. Skrupskelis and Elizabeth M. Berkeley. Charlottesville: University Press of Virginia, 1992–2004.

James, William. *Essays in Philosophy.* Cambridge, Mass.: Harvard University Press, 1978.

James, William. *Essays in Radical Empiricism.* 1912. Reprint, Cambridge, Mass.: Harvard University Press, 1976.

James, William. *Principles of Psychology.* 1890. Reprint, New York: Dover, 1950.

James, William. *Some Problems of Philosophy.* Cambridge, Mass.: Harvard University Press, 1979.

James, William. "What Is an Emotion?" *Mind* 9, no. 34 (1884): 188–205.

Johnson, Christopher. "'French' Cybernetics." *French Studies: A Quarterly Review* 69, no. 1 (2015): 60–78.

Johnson, Christopher. *System and Writing in the Philosophy of Jacques Derrida.* Cambridge: Cambridge University Press, 1993.

Keller, Evelyn Fox. "Organisms, Machines, and Thunderstorms: A History of Self-Organization, Part One." *Historical Studies in the Natural Sciences* 38, no. 1 (2008): 45–75.

Keller, Evelyn Fox. "Organisms, Machines, and Thunderstorms: A History of Self-Organization, Part Two. Complexity, Emergence, and Stable Attractors." *Historical Studies in the Natural Sciences* 39, no. 1 (2009): 1–31.

Kuhn, Thomas. "Logic of Discovery or Psychology of Research?" In *Criticism and the Growth of Knowledge: Volume 4. Proceedings of the International Colloquium in the Philosophy of Science, London, 1965,* edited by Imre Lakatos and Alan Musgrave, 1–23. Cambridge: Cambridge University Press, 1970.

Kuhn, Thomas. *The Structure of Scientific Revolutions.* Chicago: University of Chicago Press, 1962.

Lacan, Jacques. *La Psychanalyse. 1. Travaux des Années 1953–1955.* Paris: Presses Universitaires de France, 1956.

Lafontaine, Céline. "The Cybernetic Matrix of 'French Theory.'" *Theory, Culture, and Society* 24, no. 5 (2007): 27–46.

Laplanche, Jean, and Jean-Bertrand Pontalis. *The Language of Psychoanalysis.* Translated by Donald Nicholson-Smith. New York: Hogarth Press, 1973. Original French publication 1967.

Lashley, Karl. "Physiological Analysis of the Libido." *Psychological Review* 31, no. 3 (1924): 192–202.

Latour, Bruno. *An Inquiry into Modes of Existence: An Anthropology of the Moderns.* Translated by Catherine Porter. Cambridge, Mass.: Harvard University Press, 2013.

LeDoux, Joseph. *Anxious: Using the Brain to Understand and Treat Fear and Anxiety.* New York: Viking, 2015.

Leo, Russ. "An Archive for Affect Theory." *Reviews in Cultural Theory* 2, no. 2 (2011): 1–9.

Levinson, Marjorie. "A Motion and a Spirit: Romancing Spinoza." *Studies in Romanticism* 46, no. 4 (2007): 367–408.

Leys, Ruth. *The Ascent of Affect: Genealogy and Critique.* Chicago: Chicago University Press, 2017.

Lindeman, Marjaana, and Minna Sirelius. "Food Choice Ideologies: The Modern Manifestations of Normative and Humanist Views of the World." *Appetite* 37, no. 3 (2001): 175–84.

Liu, Lydia. "The Cybernetic Unconscious: Rethinking Lacan, Poe, and French Theory." *Critical Inquiry* 36, no. 2 (2010): 288–320.

Love, Heather A. "Cybernetic Modernism and the Feedback Loop: Ezra Pound's Poetics of Transmission." *Modernism/Modernity* 23, no. 1 (2016): 89–111.

Malabou, Catherine. *What Should We Do with Our Brain?* New York: Fordham University Press, 2008.

Massumi, Brian. *Parables for the Virtual: Movement, Affect, Sensation.* Durham, N.C.: Duke University Press, 2002.

Miller, George. "The Magic Number Seven, Plus or Minus Two: Some Limits on Our Capacity for Processing Information." *Psychological Review* 63, no. 2 (1956): 81–97.

Montag, Warren, and Ted Stolze, eds. *The New Spinoza.* Minneapolis: University of Minnesota Press, 1997.

Mosher, Donald, and James Sullivan. "Sexual Polarity Scale." In *Handbook of Sexuality-Related Measures*, edited by Terri D. Fisher, Clive M. Davis, William L. Yarber, and Sandra L. Davis, 415–19. New York: Routledge, 1998.

Mosher, Donald, and Silvan Tomkins. "Scripting the Macho Man: Hypermasculine Socialization and Enculturation." *Journal of Sex Research* 25, no. 1 (1988): 60–84.

Muller, John, and William Richardson, eds. *The Purloined Poe: Lacan, Derrida, and Psychoanalytic Reading*. Baltimore: Johns Hopkins University Press, 1988.

Murray, Henry. *Explorations in Personality: A Clinical and Experimental Study of Fifty Men of College Age*. New York: John Wiley, 1938.

Murray, Henry. "What Should Psychologists Do about Psychoanalysis?" *Journal of Abnormal and Social Psychology* 35, no. 2 (1940): 150–75.

Nathanson, Donald. "A Timetable for Shame." In *The Many Faces of Shame*, edited by Donald Nathanson, 1–63. New York: Guilford Press, 1987.

Ngai, Sianne. *Ugly Feelings*. Cambridge, Mass.: Harvard University Press, 2009.

Panksepp, Jaak, and Lucy Biven. *The Archaeology of Mind: Neuroevolutionary Origins of Human Emotions*. New York: W. W. Norton, 2012.

Papoulias, Constantina, and Felicity Callard. "Biology's Gift: Interrogating the Turn to Affect." *Body and Society* 16, no. 1 (2010): 29–56.

Pickering, Andrew. *The Cybernetic Brain: Sketches of Another Future*. Chicago: University of Chicago Press, 2010.

Proceedings of the Fourteenth International Congress of Psychology: Montreal— June 1954. Actes du Quatorzième Congrès International de Psychologie. Amsterdam: North-Holland, 1955.

Roazen, Paul. "Interviews on Freud and Jung with Henry A. Murray in 1965." *Journal of Analytical Psychology* 48 (2003): 1–27.

Roudinesco, Elisabeth. *Jacques Lacan & Co.: A History of Psychoanalysis in France, 1925–1985*. Translated by Jeffrey Mehlman. Chicago: University of Chicago Press, 1990.

Saint-Amour, Paul, ed. "Weak Theory." Special issue. *Modernism/Modernity* 25, no. 3 (2018).

Santayana, George. "The Ethical Doctrine of Spinoza." *The Harvard Monthly*, no. 2 (June 1886): 144–52.

Schachter, Stanley, and Jerome Singer. "Cognitive, Social, and Physiological Determinants of Emotional State." *Psychological Review* 69, no. 5 (1962): 379–99.

Scherer, Klaus, and Paul Ekman, eds. *Approaches to Emotion*. Hillsdale, N.J.: Erlbaum, 1984.

Sedgwick, Eve Kosofsky. *Epistemology of the Closet*. Berkeley: University of California Press, 1990.

Sedgwick, Eve Kosofsky. "Melanie Klein and the Difference Affect Makes." *South Atlantic Quarterly* 106, no. 3 (2007): 625–42.

Sedgwick, Eve Kosofsky. "Paranoid Reading and Reparative Reading; or, You're So Paranoid, You Probably Think This Introduction Is about You." In *Novel Gazing: Queer Readings in Fiction*, edited by Eve Kosofsky Sedgwick, 1–37. Durham, N.C.: Duke University Press, 1997.

Sedgwick, Eve Kosofsky. *Touching Feeling: Affect, Pedagogy, Performativity*. Durham, N.C.: Duke University Press, 2003.

Sedgwick, Eve Kosofsky, and Adam Frank, eds. *Shame and Its Sisters: A Silvan Tomkins Reader*. Durham, N.C.: Duke University Press, 1995.

Sedgwick, Eve Kosofsky, and Adam Frank. "Shame in the Cybernetic Fold: Reading Silvan Tomkins." In *Shame and Its Sisters: A Silvan Tomkins Reader*, 1–28. Durham, N.C.: Duke University Press, 1995.

Spinoza, Benedict. *A Spinoza Reader: The Ethics and Other Works*. Edited and translated by Edwin Curley. Princeton, N.J.: Princeton University Press, 1994.

Stern, Daniel. *The Interpersonal World of the Infant*. New York: Basic Books, 1985.

Tomkins, Silvan. "Affect and the Psychology of Knowledge." In *Affect, Cognition and Personality: Empirical Studies*, edited by Silvan Tomkins and Carroll Izard, 72–97. New York: Springer, 1965.

Tomkins, Silvan. *Affect Imagery Consciousness: Volume 1. The Positive Affects*. New York: Springer, 1962.

Tomkins, Silvan. *Affect Imagery Consciousness: Volume 2. The Negative Affects*. New York: Springer, 1963.

Tomkins, Silvan. *Affect Imagery Consciousness: Volume 3. The Negative Affects: Anger and Fear*. New York: Springer, 1991.

Tomkins, Silvan. *Affect Imagery Consciousness: Volume 4. Cognition: Duplication and Transformation of Information*. New York: Springer, 1992.

Tomkins, Silvan. "Affect Theory." In *Emotion in the Human Face*, 2nd ed., edited by Paul Ekman, 353–95. Cambridge: Cambridge University Press, 1982.

Tomkins, Silvan. "An Analysis of the Use of Electric Shock with Human Subjects." *Journal of Psychology* 15, no. 2 (1943): 285–97.

Tomkins, Silvan. "Conscience, Self Love and Benevolence in the System of Bishop Butler." PhD diss., University of Pennsylvania, 1934.

Tomkins, Silvan. "Consciousness and the Unconscious in a Model of the Human Being." In *Proceedings of the Fourteenth International Congress of Psychology: Montreal—June 1954. Actes du Quatorzième Congrès International de Psychologie,* 160–61. Amsterdam: North-Holland, 1955.

Tomkins, Silvan. "Experimental Study of Anxiety." *Journal of Psychology* 15, no. 2 (1943): 307–13.

Tomkins, Silvan. "Inverse Archeology: Facial Affect and the Interfaces of Scripts within and between Persons." In *Exploring Affect: The Selected Writings of Silvan S. Tomkins,* edited by E. Virginia Demos, 284–90. Cambridge: Cambridge University Press, 1995.

Tomkins, Silvan S. "La Conscience et L'Inconscient Représentés dans un Modèle de L'Être Humain." In *La Psychoanalyse. 1. Travaux des Années 1953–1955,* translated by Muriel Cahen, edited by Jacques Lacan, 275–86. Paris: Presses Universitaires de France, 1956.

Tomkins, Silvan. "Left and Right: A Basic Dimension of Ideology and Personality." In *The Study of Lives: Essays on Personality in Honor of Henry A. Murray,* edited by Robert White, 389–411. New York: Atherton, 1963.

Tomkins, Silvan. "A Modified Model of Smoking Behavior." In *Smoking, Health, and Behavior,* edited by Edgar Borgatta and Robert Evans, 165–86. Chicago: Aldine, 1968.

Tomkins, Silvan. "Personality Research and Psychopathology: A Commentary." In *Perspectives in Personality Research,* edited by Henry David and J. C. Brengelmann, 150–58. New York: Springer, 1960.

Tomkins, Silvan. "Personality Theory and Social Science." In *Interdisciplinary Relationships in the Social Sciences,* edited by Muzafer Sherif and Carolyn Sherif, 197–208. Chicago: Aldine, 1969.

Tomkins, Silvan. "Personology Is a Complex, Lifelong, Never-Ending Enterprise." *Personality and Social Psychology Bulletin* 8, no. 4 (1982): 608–11.

Tomkins, Silvan. *Polarity Scale.* New York: Springer, 1964.

Tomkins, Silvan. "Psychological Model for Smoking Behavior." *American Journal of Public Health* 56, no. 12 (1966): 17–20.

Tomkins, Silvan. "The Psychology of Commitment. Part 1: The Constructive Role of Violence and Suffering for the Individual and for His Society." In *Affect, Cognition, and Personality: Empirical Studies,* edited by Silvan Tomkins and Carroll Izard, 148–71. New York: Springer, 1965.

Tomkins, Silvan. "The Quest for Primary Motives: Biography and Autobiography of an Idea." *Journal of Personality and Social Psychology* 41, no. 2 (1981): 306–29.

Tomkins, Silvan. "The Rise, Fall, and Resurrection of the Study of Personality." *The Journal of Mind and Behavior* 2, no. 4 (1981): 443–52.

Tomkins, Silvan. "Script Theory." In *The Emergence of Personality,* edited by Joel Aronoff, Albert Rabin, and Robert Zucker, 147–216. New York: Springer, 1987.

Tomkins, Silvan. "Script Theory: Differential Magnification of Affects." In *Nebraska Symposium on Motivation—1978,* vol. 26, edited by Herbert Howe and Richard Dienstbier, 201–36. Lincoln: University of Nebraska Press, 1979.

Tomkins, Silvan. "Some Varieties of Psychological Organization." In *The Reach of Mind: Essays in Memory of Kurt Goldstein,* edited by Marianne Simmel, 219–30. New York: Springer, 1968.

Tomkins, Silvan, with Elizabeth Tomkins. *The Thematic Apperception Test: The Theory and Technique of Interpretation.* New York: Grune and Stratton, 1947.

Tomkins, Silvan, and Robert McCarter. "What and Where Are the Primary Affects? Some Evidence for a Theory." *Perceptual and Motor Skills* 18, no. 1 (1964): 119–58.

Tomkins, Silvan, and Samuel Messick, eds. *Computer Simulation of Personality: Frontier of Psychological Theory.* New York: John Wiley, 1963.

Tomkins, Silvan, and John Miner. *The Tomkins–Horn Picture Arrangement Test.* New York: Springer, 1957.

Triplet, Rodney. "Harvard Psychology, the Psychological Clinic, and Henry A. Murray: A Case Study in the Establishment of Disciplinary Boundaries." In *Science at Harvard University: Historical Perspectives,* edited by Clark Elliott and Margaret Rossiter, 223–50. Bethlehem, Pa.: Lehigh University Press, 1992.

Watson, John B., and Rosalie Rayner. "Conditioned Emotional Reactions." *Journal of Experimental Psychology* 3, no. 1 (1920): 1–14.

Westen, Drew. *The Political Brain: The Role of Emotion in Deciding the Fate of the Nation.* New York: Public Affairs, 2007.

White, Robert. *The Study of Lives: Essays on Personality in Honor of Henry A. Murray.* New York: Atherton, 1963.

Wiener, Norbert. *Cybernetics; or, Control and Communication in the Animal and the Machine.* 1948. Reprint, Cambridge, Mass.: MIT Press, 1965.

Wiener, Norbert. *The Human Use of Human Beings.* Boston: Houghton Mifflin, 1950.

Wilson, Edward O. *Consilience: The Unity of Knowledge.* New York: Vintage, 1998.

Wilson, Elizabeth A. *Affect and Artificial Intelligence.* Seattle: University of Washington Press, 2010.

Wilson, Elizabeth A. *Neural Geographies: Feminism and the Microstructure of Cognition.* New York: Routledge, 1998.

Wolstein, Benjamin. "The Romantic Spinoza in America." *Journal of the History of Ideas* 14, no. 3 (1953): 439–50.

INDEX

Page numbers in italics refer to figures.

Adam J. Frank is professor in the Department of English Language and Literatures at the University of British Columbia, Vancouver. He is the author of *Transferential Poetics, from Poe to Warhol* and coeditor (with Eve Kosofsky Sedgwick) of *Shame and Its Sisters: A Silvan Tomkins Reader.*

Elizabeth A. Wilson is Samuel Candler Dobbs Professor of Women's, Gender, and Sexuality Studies at Emory University. She is the author of *Gut Feminism*; *Affect and Artificial Intelligence*; *Psychosomatic: Feminism and the Neurological Body*; and *Neural Geographies: Feminism and the Microstructure of Cognition.*